RESILIENCE

From Shavl to Southfield via Dachau

Samuel Pruchno's story
as told by his daughter
MARCIA PRUCHNO LAWRENCE

Copyright © 2011 Marcia Pruchno Lawrence
All rights reserved.
ISBN: 1460913183
ISBN-13: 9781460913185

For my Dad,
For my son,
And for all the generations to come...

CONTENTS

Prologue	1
Introduction	3
Shavl—Childhood	9
Shavl—the Russians (Soviets, Communists)	37
Shavl—the Germans (Nazis)	46
Shavl—Ghettos	52
Stutthof	73
Dachau	80
Death March	96
Icking	104
Munich	119
Atlantic Ocean	153
Detroit	157
Northville	183
Dachau—Visited	192
Southfield	199
Dachau—Revisited	204
Southfield—Retirement	211
The Conversation	220
The Blessing	222
The Descendants	224
Epilogue	230
Dad's Reading Recommendations	239
Acknowledgements	241

PROLOGUE

The Holocaust was the systematic annihilation of European Jewry orchestrated by Nazi Germany during WWII, the military conflict that involved most of the world's nations between 1939 and 1945. Germany's depraved leader, Adolph Hitler, opened the floodgates of anti-Semitism that existed throughout Europe for a millennium, among all strata of society, from farmers to doctors and clerks to lawyers. For without the acquiescence, if not wholehearted cooperation, of a great number of Europeans, the Nazis could not have implemented what they referred to as their "Final Solution to the Jewish Question." Being from Lithuania, my Dad and his family were caught in this maelstrom of savagery where two thirds of the Jewish population of Europe was murdered—a total of six million Jews, including members of his own family.

INTRODUCTION

My Dad, a Holocaust Survivor, asked me why I wanted to write his story. Let me begin by saying I am not a writer but an architect. I typically write in phrases, not sentences. In fact, until recently I hated writing; it was my least favorite subject in school, a long time ago. But in 2001, when my son Max was nine-months-old, we moved into our "new" house—a highly renovated (i.e. gutted) version of the house my husband Eli grew up in. Concurrently we moved into the 21st century and bought a computer, ostensibly so I could work from home. And so I began my "Max Diaries," typical stuff, I wrote about the adorable things he said and did. It didn't take long before I realized that if I could do it for my son—I could also do it for my Dad.

There is no one answer as to why I wanted to write Dad's story, although the obvious answer is for Max. Max is Dad's only biological grandchild. And by the time Max is old enough to hear his Grandpa's stories first hand, Dad may not be in a position to tell them. Max is growing up a very privileged boy, just like his Grandpa did (I'm not saying I didn't), but the history of the Jews is cyclical. At times we peacefully coexist with our neighbors, and at other times we endure Crusades, pogroms, the Inquisition, and worse. Usually the cycle takes a few hundred years, and after the Holocaust we Jews should be O.K. for a few more generations. But at the rate at which people can kill each other these days that time frame may be compressed. I worry for Max's future in a world gone crazy. I want Max to know, and to feel deep down in his very soul, from what strong stock he comes.

The second answer is that Dad's generation is dying out. Soon there will be no one left who can say, "I am a Survivor." I say this with a capital "S," because when I was growing up the word "Survivor" meant one thing and one thing only—that a person survived the Holocaust. Today the word is used for cancers and car crashes, not that those aren't horrible things, but one is a natural course of life and the other is accidental—the Holocaust was something else entirely. Not only do I want Max to have his Grandpa's story, but our family and friends as well, so they too can pass his eyewitness account on to their children. I firmly believe that anyone with a connection to Dad, however remote, will want to read his story.

These days Dad lectures to children and adults on a regular basis at the Holocaust Memorial Center in Farmington Hills, Michigan. He also lectures at schools and synagogues in the metro-Detroit area. Dad began lecturing as he read in the media about more and more people denying the Holocaust ever happened. He just couldn't keep silent and let the truth be buried along with his relatives. I have not heard his lectures myself, but my understanding from others who have, is that Dad leaves them begging for more. And when Dad declines an invitation because it's too far for him to drive, a chauffeur is arranged. Dad has also lectured at TACOM LCMC (Tank-Automotive and Armaments Command), and even at Ford Motor Co., which is ironic since Henry Ford, the founder, was a big time anti-Semite. I've read Dad's fan mail (yes, the teachers still require the students write thank-you notes), and those letters reveal that Dad has touched the hearts and minds of many children.

My final answer to Dad's question about why I wanted to write his story is—I did it for me. While I was growing up, Dad never talked about the Holocaust, instead, he gave me books to read. He didn't talk about his life beforehand or after. I went to Hebrew school three times a week, taught mostly by Survivors, and heard everybody else's story, but not his. I had no feeling for the people in his life, his parents (my grandparents), his sister (the aunt for whom I'm named), or needless to say, any of his other relatives. He never brought it up, so I didn't either. I was afraid, not of what I might hear, but that it would be too painful for him to revisit that time and place. Then in the early 1980s, he and his brother Al went to the Survivor's Reunion in Israel. Afterward, I thought, if he could do that, then he could talk to me.

So one Sunday afternoon I worked up the courage, interrupted his sun bathing with the newspaper, and asked him those questions that had occupied my brain for as long as I could remember. The first thing Dad said to me was classic, "I didn't think you were interested." I was dumbfounded. (He couldn't really believe that, could he?) He talked to me for hours that day and told me many stories, which I wish I had written down, but a twenty-year-old doesn't think of documentation. For me it was one of the most meaningful days of my life, not only was I connecting with my Dad, but with a part of myself.

In the years that followed I would occasionally overhear Dad tell one of the old stories or divulge a new one. However, that day in the sun was never repeated. When Dad was seventy-years-old I convinced him to do a videotape for the Spielberg Shoah Foundation, a worldwide campaign to record as many Survivors' testimonies as possible. Dad consented to do a tape, one of nearly fifty-two thousand who did, but he seemed stiff and nervous with the interviewer, not his personable self. Besides, it was limited in its scope, and there was so much more I wanted to know.

As I've gotten older I have come to the conclusion that it's terribly unfair that the responsibility for passing on his history falls to me, I'm so ill equipped for the task, being notorious for my bad memory. And so I began this project.

I pestered Dad for a good eight months before the project got off and rolling. Obviously it couldn't go anywhere without his input.

He complained that every time we spoke on the phone I would ask him if he's started our project yet. It clearly was not his most pressing endeavor. Dad began recording his first tape on January 30, 2005, but I didn't receive it until September. Then he became the one bothering me, wondering if I had caught up to him yet. As it turned out it was nice to have a project to work on together, especially since we don't live in the same city to have a day-to-day relationship.

As I have found with the practice of architecture, and it applies here as well, to understand the building, you need to draw it up; to understand the story, you need to write it down. Dad has a way of speaking with his heavy accent, mixed grammar, and unique manner of expressing himself that is very charming. "Shovel the driveway, the snow," has always been a family favorite. And "Is your finger broken?" translates to—I haven't heard from you in a while, you're so busy you can't pick up the telephone and call me? But I realized after hearing a story that has held my rapt attention, I was not sure enough of the details to repeat it.

And so, Dad would send me a tape, I would write it down. Then he'd send me another one. His thoughts were all over the place, but at least he sounded relaxed on these tapes, with no one looking over his shoulder and listening while he spoke. After all ten tapes were transcribed and organized, without embellishment, my questions answered, his clarifications made, Dad carefully went over the manuscript for accuracy. And as he proofread, he was reminded of another story, and another story. Back and forth we went, and I thought this project would never end.

Although my impetus for this undertaking was the Holocaust, I found the more I learned, the more compelled I became to continue Dad's story. It's disappointing that so many Survivors' accounts end when the war ended, when in reality that was just the beginning of their lives. How did these ordinary people, who lived through such anguish, pick themselves up and continue living and loving and doing?

Just to be clear, this book is not a work of scholarship; it's a work of my Dad's remembrance and of my love for him. I wanted to write Dad's story because my curiosity, not only for what he lived through, but how he did it, is limitless. When the cold wind blows on a winter's day and I shiver in my full-length fur coat, I wonder how my Dad endured the ghettos and the concentration camps.

SHAVL — CHILDHOOD

✹ ✹ ✹

SPRING 1927 — SPRING 1939

Samuel Pruchno, Shmuel ben Chaim Yitzchak in Hebrew, nicknamed Mulle in Yiddish, my Dad, was born on April 1, 1927, in Shavl (Siauliai), Lithuania. The family name, Pruchno, is now pronounced as it is spelled, but originally the "ch" had a guttural sound. Throughout this story I refer to my dad as Dad, whether he was five-years-old, or fifty-five, he is still my Dad. To avoid confusion, I always refer to Dad's father as Father.

Dad was the youngest of four children. He and his siblings grew up in Shavl, during the brief period between the two World Wars, when much of the map of Eastern Europe had been reconfigured, and Lithuania was a sovereign country. Prior to WWI, Lithuania was part of the Russian Empire under the last Tsar, and after WWII, it was part of the Soviet Union under the Communists. Although the numbers vary depending on the source, the Jewish community in Lithuania totaled approximately 150,000 and was renown for its learning and culture. Shavl was its third largest city with about sixty-six hundred Jews, approximately twenty percent of the general population.

Dad's brother Albert, Avraham ben Chaim Yitzchak in Hebrew, nicknamed Bumke in Yiddish, was born on May 6, 1923, and was four years older than Dad. For the majority of my childhood, Dad's brother and his family lived around the block from us in Southfield, Michigan. He was my Uncle Al, or just plain Unc.

Shavl — Childhood

The boys' older sister Maša, spelled "Marcia" in English, was born in 1919; their sister Lea Lily was born sometime between the boys. Dad remembers Lily as being older than Al, but Al relayed to his daughter Rachel that Lily was his baby sister. This being Dad's story I would have deferred to him, except for the existence of a family photograph with Maša and Al. During that time period family portraits were an event, so there would have been no reason for such a photograph to exist without Lily. Therefore, she must have been younger than Al.

Their parents were also born in "Lithuania," within a forty-mile radius of Shavl in the northern, central region. Dad's Father, Chaim Yitzchak (ben Avraham) Pruchno, was born in the town of Linkuva (as was Al). Dad's Mother, Chaya Rachel (bat Moshe) Zak, was from the small town of Pusalotas.

Dad's Father's mother, Sonia, was the only grandparent Dad had even a vague memory of; she lived with them for about a year before she died around 1933.

The Pruchno siblings didn't have many aunts, uncles or cousins. The only relative they saw from time to time was their Uncle Boris, Dad's Father's younger brother. He was married to a woman named Sonia and they had no children. They lived in Ponovezh (Panevezys), the fourth largest city in Lithuania.

The aunts and uncles on their Mother's side lived too faraway to visit; one lived in Poland and the other in America. Aunt Sonia (not to be confused with Boris's wife or Dad's grandmother) lived in Warsaw, although Dad never met her, Al had. She was married to a man named Morris Yussim and they had two sons, Solomon and Gutek. The young men had been studying (or practicing) medicine in Switzerland when they came home for a summer visit just before Germany invaded Poland in 1939, then they were prohibited from leaving the country. Dad's Mother sent care packages of food and clothing until she no longer got acknowledgements that her sister's family received them. The Yussims died in the Warsaw ghetto in 1941.

Spring 1927 — Spring 1939

Dad's Mother had a brother in Cleveland, Ohio, named Benjamin, who Dad and Al met after the war. Ben was married in Lithuania to Chana Schlossberg of Vilkomir (Ukmerge). They moved to Warsaw where their three sons were born. Ben had owned a soap factory that was conscripted by the Kaiser to manufacture gas masks during WWI. In 1921 they were "sponsored" and moved to the United States. It was their eldest son George who had convinced them to leave Poland; it was he who felt the oppressive anti-Semitism in school and on the streets. Ben was a man of means in Europe, but not in America. By the time Dad got to know him, he was an old man, a bit disheveled and legally blind. He still carried the weighted cane he had in Poland, which could double as a weapon. He died in 1957 having survived his wife by twenty-one years. Ben told Dad stories about Dad's Mother, and like me, Dad wishes he had written them down when he first heard them. He can only remember Ben saying, "Chaya Rachel was a no-nonsense kind of gal."

I have my own memories of the "Cleveland" Zaks. I not only remember Ben's sons, George, Dave and Max, but I have a deep affection for George and Max. (Dave, I barely knew.) Although they were cousins, being about fifty years older than me, I related to them as uncles. The Zak and Pruchno generations don't exactly line up; they are on their fourth generation since Chaya Rachel and Ben, while we are on our third. Besides three sons, Ben also has seven grandchildren, ten great-grandchildren, ten great great-grandchildren, and still counting. Ben's sons have died, but we Pruchnos still see some members of the Zak clan at weddings and Bar Mitzvahs.

Growing up I knew very little of my Dad's family, but still, it came as a surprise when Dad announced he was putting up a memorial plaque for his sister in shul. I thought he had lost

Shavl — Childhood

his mind. I grew up seeing Maša's plaque, and from my perspective it always felt a bit eerie, because her plaque bore my name, complete with English spelling. I gently tried to remind Dad that there already exists a plaque for his sister. He dismissively waved his hand at me and said, "Not that sister! My other sister!" What other sister, I wondered? Until that moment I thought Dad was one of three children, not four. How could it be that he never mentioned her before? When war turns life upside down and inside out, can a person really forget—a sister?

Dad's "other" sister, Lily, was a very good-looking girl, but so was the rest of the family as evidenced by the old photographs. Lily was about seven-years-old when she died of a childhood illness on September 16, 1932. (Dad and Al were not sure of this date, "it was still warmish outside," but they needed an anniversary on which to say Kaddish, the mourner's prayer praising God.) On the day of her funeral Dad was left behind with the maid. He screamed and cried and carried on because he thought he was missing something, but at five-years-old, his parents thought he was just too young to go to a cemetery. All he remembers was that there were a lot of people in the house for Shiva, the seven-day period of mourning, and that the reins on his behavior were loosened quite a bit. Later, whenever Dad would ask his Mother about Lily, she would cry. So Dad stopped asking—and began forgetting her.

Dad's parents built a new stucco clad brick house at No. 20 Rudes Street, which they moved into shortly after Lily's death. It was about a fifteen-minute walk from the center of town, in a predominately Jewish area. That said, their immediate neighbors were a gentile businessman and his family on one side; and a priest, his niece, and a group of nuns in a large two story house on the other side.

Spring 1927 — Spring 1939

Dad's family lived in the house for about two years until one October night, Maša's girlfriend, who was sleeping over, returned from a date just in time to alert the family to a potentially catastrophic situation. The house was on fire! Dad's Mother, dressed in her robe and slippers, threw Dad over her shoulder, grabbed Al by the hand, and quickly escorted them out of harm's way to a neighbor's house. Dad is still amazed she had the strength to carry him. (Being a somewhat petite mother myself, I'm not as easily impressed.) She then rejoined her husband and daughter to watch the blaze. Even though the firefighters poured a lot of water into the house, the roof and a portion of the second floor could not be saved. Thankfully no one lived upstairs at the time. Dad's parents had insurance, and the crew that originally built their house, rebuilt the damaged portions, with one important modification—a sheet metal roof. (The fire had begun at the juncture between the roof and the hot water heater flue.) In the meantime, the Pruchnos rented an apartment not far from the house.

One evening while living in the apartment, his Mother gave Al money to take Dad along with him and his friend to a movie; she was busy and needed Dad occupied. (As they got older Al continued to take Dad to the movies, on the condition that Dad pay for him as well.) While they were out, Dad started to feel sick and wanted to go home. But he was afraid to walk back in the dark by himself, with God knows who or what lurking behind the bushes and trees. Al was with his friend and didn't want to be bothered with his baby brother; instead, he bought Dad an ice cream to shut him up. Dad didn't refuse the ice cream, but he ate it shivering. When they got home Dad complained to his Mother that he felt queasy. She felt his feverish forehead and then took his temperature—it was very high. That night Dad slept with his parents.

The next morning the Doctor came by, and he must have told Dad's parents that their boy was very sick, because Dad stayed in bed for two months and remained in the house for another month as well. He never slept alone; one night his Mother slept with him and the next night his Father. They were constantly taking his temperature and putting cold compresses on his forehead. The Doctor would come, sometimes twice a day, and stick a tongue depressor down Dad's throat, which only increased Dad's nausea. Maša and Al stayed away, but when Dad felt better they would stand by the door and talk to him. To encourage Dad's recovery his parents bought him all kinds of toys, anything he wanted, including a fireman's helmet. Whatever illness Dad had, he completely recovered from; it may have been scarlet fever. Only then did his Father take him to see the reconstruction of their house.

The house was completed that summer of 1935, and Dad's parents threw a big party for all the workers and neighbors. They ate and drank the entire evening. They also put a wreath on top of the roof, a custom for good luck.

The house sat on a large lot that measured about three hundred feet across, with a white picket fence all around. The ground was bare dirt (no grass lawns of today), the walks were cement tiles, and the street was made of cobblestones. When facing the house there were evergreens along the front and a big tree to the left. Some fruit trees and strawberry bushes were to the right, in a separate fenced-in area.

I had grown up with a story about Unc and strawberries. He wouldn't touch them. One day he picked a few too many with Maša, ate them all and got sick. So in memory of his sister, he adamantly refused to eat them, ever again.

In the summertime Dad's Father would spend his evenings, after a nap and dinner, working in the garden. He was especially

Spring 1927 — Spring 1939

attentive to the fruit trees (cherry, apple and pear) and would consult an agronomist if they were not looking healthy, to ensure they survived the winter. The winters in Shavl were colder than in the mid-western United States, and there was a lot of snow. The summers were similar though, and at the back of the house Dad's Mother had a beautiful flower garden, in the middle of which was a gazebo where the family dined. According to Dad, her garden was the loveliest around.

Behind the garden there was a smaller house, built with the leftover wood materials from the construction of the main house. They rented that house to a Jewish family with a girl Dad's age. In addition, there was another building on the property, made of concrete, which housed both the chicken coop and the laundry, separated by a wall, each with its own entrance.

The laundry was a big room with a large basin in its center, over three feet in diameter. It was used for bed sheets, curtains and the like. Clothing was done in the house. All the laundry was washed, boiled, scrubbed on a board, and ironed with a hefty metal iron. Four to six times a year Dad's parents hired an additional maid to do the big, heavy laundry, because it was too much for the live-in maid.

Having a live-in maid was common then, and over the years the Pruchnos had three of them. The first one was with them for a long time. Dad played with her, and ran to her when he hurt himself. She was a gentile and would take him to church (with his Mother's permission), and Dad would stand behind the big door and watch her pray. She used to bake special cookies for Christmas. And she was the one who helped Dad's family when they were "resettled" in the ghetto.

Near the gazebo was an unusual type of swing. It consisted of a platform, rather than a seat, and all three Pruchno kids could sit or stand on it at once. Like kids everywhere, Dad had the best time by swinging as high as he could and jumping off, and he stubbornly refused to cry when he hurt himself. Beyond the swing were stacks of wood, a well (used to water the garden only), and a doghouse.

Dad was about eight-years-old when they got their dog Mufti. Al named him after the Grand Mufti of Jerusalem. The Grand Mufti was the preeminent, anti-British, anti-Jewish power in Palestine, and as far as Al was concerned, it was good to have the Mufti at their beck and call. Dad doesn't remember what type of dog he was, but he was of medium size and brown in color, with white patches on his face and forelegs. Mufti was active, always barking and running, but he was gentle too, a real family pet. They only had him for a couple of years, until one day he was run over by a car. Afterward they got another dog, a St. Bernard, but it was big and mean. It was kept on a leash in the backyard, for protection, and it slept in the doghouse. Dad's Father fed it, and he was the only one who could really control it. Dad tried to play with it once and almost got his hand bitten off. The dog died of natural causes a couple of years later.

Dad explained in great detail about the grounds, but I had to pry information from him about the house itself, as though he had forgotten that as an architect I would find that interesting. In addition to the rental unit in the backyard, there were two other rental units and they were both part of the main house. There was a unit upstairs where an elderly couple lived, and on the ground floor to the left (as viewed from the street), there was a unit where the school principal's brother lived with his family. The largest unit, the one the Pruchnos lived in, was to the right.

Their "house" was entered through an enclosed veranda directly to the living room, which was one of two rooms (besides the kitchen) with a wood-burning stove. Next was the dining room, and then Dad's parent's bedroom, which had the other stove. All these rooms were arranged along the front of the house. At the back of the house was the kitchen with the maid's room adjacent, Dad and Al's bedroom off the living room, and Maša's off their room. Maša's bedroom was larger than the boys' and had windows on two walls. It contained a bed, couch, chairs and two desks. One desk was an executive type, which held a typewriter, and that was where Dad's Father wrote his personal correspondence. When he was young, Dad loved the sound of the typewriter, and occasionally his Father would let him give it a try. Underneath the stairs to the second floor unit was a storage room where they kept the food they bought in bulk, such as flour, sugar and salt—Dad's Mother baked a lot. There was indoor plumbing, but only a cold-water tap; the hot water heater was used for bath water only. There was electricity, but no telephone. They had no car. In the whole city there were perhaps five privately owned cars, and no horse and buggies. When they were still in their house on Vilna Street they had a baby grand piano. But Maša wasn't interested in playing it, and neither were the boys, and because it took up so much room their parents sold it.

Dad reminded me that I didn't get off so easily. When I was about twelve-years-old I declared I was quitting piano lessons. Dad bellowed that he and Mom would decide when I quit. Then he took off his belt, put the ends together, snapped it to make a threatening noise, and hit a pillow. And so I sat down to practice, crying and playing, playing and crying. A couple of years later, after having had a great time playing the piano with my friends all gathered around me singing, I went up to Dad, gave him a kiss on the cheek, and thanked him for not letting me quit.

Dad's Father was the Vice President of a bank. Sometimes he would take Dad along when he needed to stop in and sign a letter. Dad enjoyed going, the employees were happy to see him, and he got to listen to a symphony of typewriters. Dad's Father was an extremely educated man. He had gone to university in

Konigsberg, Germany (now Kaliningrad, Russia), and spoke several languages—German, Russian, English, Latin, Lithuanian and Yiddish. But his Yiddish was spoken with a heavy German accent, which embarrassed Dad in front of his friends. (Over half a century later, Dad still sounds like he just got off the boat.)

Before WWI Dad's parents lived in Moscow. His Father had landed an important position there, either in manufacturing or in the import/export business. They left in 1917, when the Communists overthrew the Tsar and began the Russian Revolution. Communist doctrine demanded public ownership of all property. In such a society, Dad's parents feared that not only would their wealth be taken from them, but that they might be taken to Siberia for the crime of "capitalism."

At some point Dad's Father had even come to New York and stayed for over a year. When Dad was growing up, he would speak about the wonders of New York City, of the trains running not only above but also below the ground, and of the buildings that touched the sky. Dad just could not imagine trains running underground, nor could he visualize the high-rise buildings, since the tallest buildings in his world were only four stories high. Dad's Father's had enjoyed many concerts while in the States; his favorite piece of music from that time was *Tales of Hoffman* by Offenbach. When he played the piece on the gramophone he would hum along, and his children had to keep quiet.

Dad would later come to wonder, both during and after the war, how his life would have been different had his Father decided to stay in the United States.

Dad's Father inherited some farmland from his father, in Pamusha, approximately six miles from his hometown of Linkuva. Pamusha was a village with a dozen or so Jewish farmers. There was a very small and uncomfortable shul, with too many flies and smelly kerosene lamps that didn't give off enough light. Dad's

Spring 1927 — Spring 1939

family spent a week there during two summers, when Dad was six and seven-years-old. Some of the Jewish farmers were so poor, that comparatively, the Jews of *Fiddler on the Roof* lived in luxury.

Across from their land was a Jewish farmer named Mordechai, who was about forty-years-old. He was a good-hearted man who proved to be extremely kind to Dad's family, and especially to Dad. Mordechai lived with his brother, sister-in-law and their grown daughter, in a house with a dirt floor and a non-working chimney. When his sister-in-law cooked, smoke filled the house. Once a year Mordechai would come to Shavl with his wagon to sell his produce at the open market, and he would stay with Dad's family. Although Dad's parents rented their land to a gentile farmer, they had an agreement that Mordechai could access drinking water from their well, since his own water was only fit for the animals.

Dad and Al enjoyed being on the farm; the big thrill was the horses. In the evenings the tenant farmers would let the boys ride them to the river for washing. They would put Al on the front and Dad on the back, and of course, Al always got to hold the reins. One day Dad insisted on having his own horse. But when the horse shook his belly, Dad fell to the ground. From then on, Dad was fine riding with his brother. On one occasion Dad and Al helped transport manure from the stables to the fields. They sat in the wagon and guided the horses, but they got smelly and dirty, and in a lot of trouble when they got home. They certainly felt it when their Mother's heavy gold wedding ring hit them, and the mark stayed a good long time. It took her hours to clean them up, and their manure caked shoes were ruined. But how they loved the horses.

Twice, when Dad was four and five-years-old, his family summered in the resort town of Palanga on the Baltic Sea. They went with another family who had a boy Dad's age. The only part Dad didn't enjoy about those summers was that his Mother insisted they go to the sea everyday, regardless of the weather. Luckily the water wasn't too cold. If the seas were rough and the waves were big, she would simply hold their hands. She was a strong swimmer, but the sea wasn't the best place for swimming instruction. Since it was quite a long train ride, Dad's Father would only be able to join them for three or four weekends during the course of the summer. Then he would go to the beach, lie on his back, and read the newspaper.

Some summers they went to Tzitevian (Tytuvenai), a village not far from Shavl, about an hour away to the south, which was more convenient for Dad's Father. They stayed in a big cottage that they shared with another family, in a wooded area with plenty of room to play. Dad couldn't recall if there was a little lake there or not. One summer his Mother hired a tutor, who was also vacationing there, to help Dad with his Hebrew. Dad was tutored along with another boy from his class, Shimon Blank.

Dad admits to being a little spoiled, but attributes it to his ranking as the youngest. His Mother had to bribe him with treats from the bakery in order to get the grocery shopping done. When Dad was young, about five or six-years-old, he was a very picky eater. (I did not give him such grief; I ate just about everything.) The only thing he would eat for dinner was white hamburger, made from chicken, and it had to be a certain color. His potato, sliced and fried, also had to be a certain color. His chicken soup had to be clear; if there were carrots floating around, Dad was not eating it, and there was no way his Mother could resurrect it. Now he wonders how she put up with all that nonsense.

Once he got a little older and started ice-skating, Dad would come home ravenous, and then there was nothing he wouldn't

Spring 1927 — Spring 1939

eat, including whole meals his Mother had prepared to serve the entire family. Eventually she had to resort to hiding them. Dad still remembers his Mother's holiday specialties—gribenes (cracklings) and shmaltz (chicken fat) with salami and challah for Shabbat, homentashen (pastry) for Purim, and stuffed kneydl (dumpling) and tayglach (pastry) for Pesach. Dad has not tasted better tayglach to this day. Of course, nothing can compare to the delicacies of childhood.

The holidays in Dad's house were always exciting. His Mother would start preparing for Pesach two months prior. She would take the children to the tailor, where they would get new school uniforms, suits, shirts, and short pants (when they were younger) or knickers with long socks (when they were older). It required three fittings. Two weeks before Pesach she would hire extra help; it was too much for the live-in maid even with working longer hours. Everything needed to be cleaned, washed or polished—it was a big production. After certain areas of the house were finished, they couldn't be used again until the holiday. When Pesach finally arrived, the Seder table was laden with silver. There was a special tray engraved in Russian, with a decanter and a dozen cups, the outside of the cups were silver and the inside gold. The set had been a going-away present from Dad's Father's work when he had left Moscow. Dad thought it was magnificent.

Then there were the Shabbat candlesticks Dad's Mother lit every Friday night, they stood about two feet tall. Dad has never seen a pair quite like them again, and he's rummaged through countless silver stores since. After a wonderful meal, Dad's Father told the children stories—he was a great storyteller. Dad's favorites were Sherlock Holmes and Allan Pinkerton, both detective

Shavl — Childhood

stories. But by then it was late, and Dad was tired, and he could never quite manage to stay awake until the end. The next morning he would ask Al what happened, and Al would want to charge him for the information. Dad soon learned it was much more economical to ask his sister.

On Saturday morning they attended synagogue. It was a big, beautiful, Orthodox shul where the women sat in the balcony. Dad's Father sat in the second row. He was very serious about his davening (praying), and if his boys wanted to talk, or anyone else nearby for that matter, he'd sternly tell them to take it outside. At any given moment Dad's Father would quiz them as to where in the service the hazzan (cantor) was chanting—much like Dad did later on to my brother and me.

Afterward they came home to a lunch of petcha and cholent, and they enjoyed their day of rest. Petcha isn't for the uninitiated; it doesn't look good or sound good. It's calf's foot jelly, served cold and congealed. (This was a dish my Mom adamantly refused to make, but when her best girlfriend's mom did, she was sure to put some aside for Dad.) Cholent, on the other hand, has a more universal appeal. It is a dish of a hundred variations, which simmers overnight, and basically consists of meat, potatoes, barley and beans.

Dad's first day of kindergarten was traumatic; he screamed and cried so much his Mother had to come back for him. It took him some time to adjust. Remarkably, the majority of the kids Dad went to school with, from kindergarten through the Hebrew Gymnasium (a secondary school that prepared students for university), a class of about twenty-five, survived the war. They included Leo Bakstansky, Lily Lazarovich, Sara Matuson, Devorah Kuint, Abrasha Rotshtein, Chaya Shilansky, and Abrasha and Ella Ziv.

Dad used to ask Chaya to do his homework, and unbelievably, she would. I asked what she got in return, but Dad had no answer. One time she messed up; their notebooks had to be neatly covered with special colored paper and something happened to it. And Dad had the nerve to yell at her! She reminded him of this incident many years later, on his most recent trip to Israel.

When I was in Israel, I met some of Dad's old friends and their children. I even spent a summer at the Bakstanskys in Tel Aviv, before beginning graduate school. I worked for Esther, Leo's wife, a sabra (native Israeli), who was an architect with the Planning Department of the Kibbutzim, and I became friendly with their daughter Hilla.

Once I had the opportunity to reintroduce Dad to a landsman. In the early 1990s I went to an AIPAC (American Israel Public Affairs Committee) event, and an acquaintance of mine introduced me to an acquaintance of his—Marcia Pruchno meet Joe Mishell. Joe and I had a nice conversation, so I wasn't surprised when he called me that evening. I was, however, surprised by what he told me.

Joe's mother had gone to school with my uncle, Bumke Pruchno! From the moment Joe heard my last name it bothered him, it sounded familiar but he couldn't place it—so he called his mom. I was stunned that he knew his mom's story so well that the mere mention of the name Pruchno triggered any response at all. I asked my Dad if he remembered Pescia Feinberg. He narrowed his eyes as he thought for a moment and said, "Yeah, I think she was sweet on Al." The next time Dad visited me in Chicago we all got together for brunch. Dad and Pescia were so cute jabbering away in Yiddish. Joe translated for me, since Yiddish was my parents' and grandparents' secret language. I can't remember what they talked about, but they seemed genuinely happy to see each other. And Joe and I have remained friends ever since.

Like any pair of brothers, Dad and Al "enjoyed" their fair share of sibling rivalry. When Dad was about six-years-old, his Mother went to see a heart specialist in Warsaw and stayed with her sister Sonia. Al got to accompany her, but Dad was just too young, he would have been more of a nuisance than anything else. Dad's Mother kissed him good-bye and promised that when she returned she would bring him a present. Dad had such a tantrum that he still refers to it as his "performance." They were gone for two or three months, and she did not return empty handed. Dad received a beautiful, realistic, fireman's helmet, complete with tassel. Al, however, was always taunting him—Warsaw was so nice, and the synagogue was so beautiful, and on and on.

Once the boys were sick in bed for a week. What started as a pillow fight, ended as a food fight, with applesauce on the beds and on the walls. They blamed each other, and Dad honestly can't remember who started it. But their Mother was extremely upset, she yelled at them and spanked them, and they knew they deserved it. After they cleaned up, she threatened—if that ever happened again they would be sent away to reform school. All the same they were relieved, for she was the gentle one, and she did not tell their Father.

Then there was the time Al wanted to teach Dad to swim. Typically their Father took them to the man-made lake, about a thirty-minute walk from their house. But on this particular occasion they went with Al's friends. Al had Dad stand in neck-deep water and then lie across his arms. He instructed Dad to move his arms and legs; then Al lowered his arms. Dad dropped like a stone to the bottom of the lake. It took Dad what seemed like an eternity to resurface, and he had swallowed a lot of water. That was the last time Dad let Al show him anything having to do with swimming.

Not long after, Al was in the school play. He had a good singing voice and got a starring role. Everyone, including his teacher, but most especially his Mother, was proud of him. It was just another reason for Dad to be envious of his big brother.

Spring 1927 — Spring 1939

Although Dad's Father didn't skate, he took Dad ice-skating. He would walk on the ice and hold Dad up, or he would sit in a special chair with runners and Dad would push him around. Dad was a quick study and in no time he was off and running (or rather gliding).

I didn't know until recently that for the first winter Dad took me ice-skating he carried me in his arms. At the beginning of the following winter he told my Mom, "If she's not letting go, she was not born to skate." Soon we were having skating contests, not for speed, but to see who fell the least number of times. Dad and I skated together until he was in his late sixties, whenever he came to Chicago for a visit. Now that I'm in my forties, I take lessons with a figure skating coach who thinks I'm a natural.

Boris, Dad's uncle, was very smart, and like Dad's Father, knew many languages, studied in Konigsberg, and had a big position in a bank (in Ponovezh). He even looked a bit like his brother, but with a little more hair, a Charlie Chaplin-like moustache, and a monocle. He wore special shoes because one foot was bigger than the other.

Whenever Uncle Boris came to visit, which was a couple of times a year, the first question Dad would ask his Mother was, "When is he leaving?" Dad had to share Maša's room with him, while Maša moved in with Al. Uncle Boris used to get up in the middle of the night and have himself a smoke. Although he never bought his niece and nephews toys, he was always generous with money.

Uncle Boris died in 1938 of a heart attack. The funeral was in Ponovezh and Dad was allowed to go. Dad and his Father took the night train to get there in time for the morning funeral. It took three to four hours, with a lot of stops, hence Dad referred to it as a "choo-choo" train. Dad had only been to his uncle's apartment one other time; it was full of books, written mostly in German. This time it was also full of flowers, sent by his gentile associates.

On their return home Dad was sad and regretted that he had always been so obnoxious to Uncle Boris. His uncle would ask him tough questions, on subjects Dad knew nothing about but clearly should have, and Dad wouldn't give him a straight answer, or he would try to avoid him altogether. Maša, on the other hand, had gotten along very well with their uncle.

Maša also got along very well with Dad. Perhaps because of the eight-year age difference, she had the patience to play with him. Dad was ten-years-old when Maša took him to his first opera, *Pagliacci,* when the Kovno Opera House came to town. (Her boyfriend was unable to attend.) Dad also used to read the books Maša was reading. She asked him why he bothered; obviously he couldn't understand them. But she was wrong—one book in particular was very sexy.

Maša would let Dad help with her school projects, if it involved something artistic. The teacher was very strict and the projects had to be perfect. Dad was a very meticulous painter. He would cover the areas that didn't receive paint, then dip a small brush in the paint and lightly run it forward and backward across a screen, before putting brush to paper. In reality, Dad didn't do too much, but he told his sister that with his help she would receive a good mark. (And with her Father's help she did very well in German; he was always correcting the teacher.)

When it came time for Maša's school conferences, Dad had to go with his Mother, all dressed up and on his best behavior. Maša always got a good report; she was smart and a good student. Their Father insisted she go to university and become an accountant, so she too could work at a bank. He felt very strongly that a young woman should have an education. If something happened to her husband and she had to support her family, she couldn't very well dig ditches. I asked Dad who chose her profession, because he and I had countless arguments about me becoming a doctor, or at least an engineer. If Dad's sister hadn't selected her profession, at least she was amenable to it.

Dad, unlike his sister, wasn't the best student, but he was good at math. Later he enjoyed inflicting it on others. Hebrew school carpools were so embarrassing; Dad would ask my friends and me math questions while driving. And I could never be sick in peace—pneumonia was no excuse. He would leave me pages and pages of math problems (God forbid I waste a minute), which he would then have to check when he came home from work, and this was before the advent of calculators. Consequently, I am also good at math.

Other subjects that interested Dad (at least some of the time) were history, geography and science. Unlike his Father, languages were not for him. (Languages were not for me either.) Dad was fascinated with the American Indians. He knew the names of the tribes and their main leaders, which ones were warriors for a just cause or just brutal killers. How the Indians handled their horses was of particular interest to him. Dad would discuss the Indians with some of his classmates and they would exchange books about them.

Dad learned to play chess from his Father, and it didn't take long before Dad could beat him. He played with Yechiel, Maša's boyfriend, and sometimes Yechiel would win and sometimes Dad would. Dad also played with Al, but Al was a sore loser, and he cheated. If Dad had to go to the bathroom mid-game, he would return to a re-arranged board.

So Dad joined the chess club at school. One day when Dad played against a team player and won, the teacher pitted him against the best team player and the game ended in a draw. From then on Dad was a member of the chess team. The team

Shavl — Childhood

was comprised of six players, Dad was ranked fifth, and at eleven or twelve-years-old he was the youngest player on the team. They played teams from other schools and also from civic organizations. One time they played the police department. The police team placed their first ranked player against Dad, an unfair tactic to gain points, but Dad won. His opponent was upset and asked to play again, just for fun. It was fun for Dad—he won again.

Being tall and muscular for his age, Dad was chosen to present a rifle to the army at the Lithuania army parade. (Dad was actually runner-up, being the next biggest in size to the boy who was home sick.) His school had collected money and bought three rifles to demonstrate their patriotism. Dad has always wondered if that rifle, which he held in his own two hands, was ever used to kill Jews.

Basically Dad was a good-hearted kid who looked for justice for everyone. He thought when he grew up he would have liked to become a doctor or a lawyer, in some way help the underprivileged. Most likely Dad's abilities would have led him to become an engineer.

When Dad was twelve-years-old, his Father bought him a full sized bicycle. Even though Maša had a deluxe model which she rarely rode; Dad couldn't possibly use hers, without the bar, it was just for girls. Dad's bicycle was gray with stripes and he was so proud of it. There was only one aspect of his bicycle he didn't like—it was made in Germany.

By this time the family had heard a few of Hitler's speeches on the radio, blaming the Jews for all Germany's troubles, including losing WWI. The Jews, he claimed, controlled the world and would soon be punished! (It was Hitler who had aspirations of world domination; he had already annexed Austria and Sudetenland the year before.) In general, Dad's parents boycotted German products (just like Dad continued to do when I was growing up), but in regards to the bicycle, nothing else was available.

Dad bought lots of gadgets for his bicycle, a front light, a speedometer, and a rack at the back. He was able to ride it right away, at least in a straight line—turning was the problem. He had to stop, get off, turn the bike around, and then get back on. Once he got the hang of it, he enjoyed riding to school. In winter Dad would take his bike almost completely apart, oil it, wrap it in special papers, and put it away to protect it from rusting. He did this for as long as he owned the bicycle, which meant until the Nazis came and took it away.

Around this time Dad's Father became ill. He had kidney stones and gallstones, problems that would plague him for the rest of his life. When he was in pain, Dad had to run to the pharmacy to pick up his medication. He always felt very bad when his Father had these attacks. Dad never let his parents know, but he was worried. What if something happened to his Father—what would happen to them?

One night Dad woke up to his parents arguing, after he had already been asleep for some time. They were having a disagreement about whether they should sell the house and its contents and move to Eretz Yisrael (the Land of Israel). His Mother didn't want to move; she didn't want to give up their house, their lifestyle, and start all over again. She remembered things being better under the more civilized Germans than under the Bolsheviks (a.k.a. Communists) during WWI. But his Father, responding to Hitler's speeches, felt it was time to leave, that there would be no future for their children in a Lithuania under German rule. Dad pushed his door ajar just in time to see his Mother open the china cabinet and ask, "Do you want to give up all this?" Their dispute went on for a few nights running and really frightened Dad. It was

Shavl — Childhood

scary enough to hear his parents argue, let alone about the subject matter. Dad didn't know what to think or whose side to take.

Another night Dad woke up screaming and crying from a terrible dream. He ran to his parent's bedroom and they calmed him down. Dad had seen a newsreel at the movies of the Spanish Civil War, bombs were dropping on civilians—children and their parents were being killed. Who could have guessed how prophetic his nightmare would become!

Spring 1927 — Spring 1939

Chaya Rachel (Zak) Pruchno
Dad's Mother.

Chaim Yitzchak Pruchno
Dad's Father.

Chaim Yitzhak & Chaya Rachel with Maša and Al
Dad's family—before Lily and Dad were born— circa 1924.

Shavl — Childhood

Sam Pruchno—Dad
*with his class—circa 1937.
standing tall, third head to the right of the window,
in a white shirt and dark jacket.*

Al Pruchno
Dad's brother standing far right, in a white shirt, with hands on hips.

Spring 1927 — Spring 1939

Maša Pruchno
with her Beitar group—1937.
Dad's sister seated to the right of the man in the center, in a dark dress.

Maša (Pruchno) Saks
Dad's sister.

Boris Pruchno
Dad's uncle.

Shavl — Childhood

Benjamin & Chana Zak with Dave, George and Max
Dad's uncle, aunt and cousins.

Sonia (Zak) & Morris Yussim with Gutek and Solomon
Dad's aunt, uncle and cousins.

Spring 1927 — Spring 1939

בשנת חיים ושלום
בכתיבה וחתימה טובה

חיים יצחק פרוכנה ומשפחתו

שבלי, רחוב רודאס 20.

Rosh Hashanah card—1930s

*To a year of life and peace.
May you be inscribed and sealed for a good year.*

Chaim Yitzchak Pruchno and family

Shavl, 20 Rudes Street

SHAVL — THE RUSSIANS (SOVIETS, COMMUNISTS)

✡ ✡ ✡

SUMMER 1939 — SUMMER 1941

In August 1939 the Soviet Union and Germany secretly signed a non-aggression treaty, whereby they divided up Northern and Eastern Europe between themselves. On the first of September the Nazis invaded Poland, the official beginning of WWII. Later that month the Communists did the same, taking their piece of Poland.

In October the Soviets established military bases in Lithuania, and in June 1940 they took control of the Baltic States—Lithuania, Latvia and Estonia. When the soldiers marched in the streets in the late afternoon they sang so powerfully they could be heard several blocks away. Dad liked to listen to them, although their songs were sometimes sad. The Russian soldiers drank a lot of vodka and smoked majorka (rough tobacco wrapped in newspaper). For fun, Dad and his friends would go to the small Russian airfield and watch the planes take off and land.

But life as they knew it had changed. The bank where Dad's Father worked, a private institution, was closed. He had to get a job elsewhere, and quickly, because if a man wasn't working he was sent to Siberia. His Father knew Russian very well, so it was relatively easy for him to find employment. A bit overqualified, he became a bookkeeper in a Russian department store. But still he worried; he owned a house and that was considered bourgeois, in other words, anti-communist.

Shavl — The Russians (Soviets, Communists)

Dad's family had to relinquish some space in their house, only so many square feet were allowed per person. During the course of the yearlong occupation they had various Russians live with them. Staying in Maša's room were two nurses (for about two months), a family of four that drank and smoked a lot (for about one month), and an air force captain (for about six months). Dad liked the Captain and even slept on the couch in his room. The Captain would sit and talk with Dad's parents for hours about how bad the living conditions were in Russia. When he was recalled he became anxious, convinced he had said something to offend someone—it did not bode well to be summoned back to Russia.

In preparation for the inevitable food shortages he remembered during WWI, Dad's Father used to bring home canned food, even though it was against the law to keep so much on hand. Dad's Mother used to complain, "Why did you buy it (whatever "it" was), it cost too much!" His Father would then tell her it was on sale. He even gave Dad money and instructed him—if ever he should see canned food, he should buy it, and tell his Mother he paid half what it actually cost. His Father warned him, "You can't eat money."

Also that year Dad's school changed from a private Hebrew Gymnasium to a public school. Some of their teachers remained the same and others were new. They could no longer be taught Hebrew, only Yiddish, and religious subjects were forbidden. The Communist ideology was atheistic. That religion became obsolete upset Dad, so he asked a lot of questions, sometimes too many. Dad was also one of just a handful of students who refused to wear the requisite red neckerchief with his white shirt. His teacher never said anything and neither did Dad. It could be dangerous to get into arguments with Communist teachers—or students for that matter.

Like Dad, Al was not the best student in class. Before the Soviets came, when he was about sixteen-years-old, his parents took him

Summer 1939 — Summer 1941

out of the Hebrew Gymnasium and enrolled him in the Technical Institute of Engineering in Kovno (Kaunas), about three hours away by train. The parents of a couple of Al's friends also sent their sons to the same school, but the majority of students at the institute were gentiles. Dad has suggested that it probably would have been his fate as well, had his education continued. Perhaps he simply preferred Al's school uniform to his own black one with its high stiff collar.

Al took learning seriously at his new school. However, he received a sum of money for living expenses, which he didn't take quite as seriously. In fact, he lost a good portion of it playing cards and barely had enough left for food. When he came home for the holidays, his Mother thought he was looking so thin because he was studying so hard. And she sent him back to school with a suitcase filled with food. Dad and his parents went to the railroad station early, to properly see Al off, but they were stopped by the Russian police conducting random searches. When the police saw the food in Al's suitcase, they wanted to arrest the Pruchnos for dealing on the black market! The family had a hard time convincing the police all that food was for personal use. Afterward, Al received much smaller packages.

When Al was home from school on vacation, he and Dad got into a huge fight, and Al beat the hell out of him. Dad confessed he didn't have the heart to hit Al that hard, and he could have, size-wise he was catching up. Al had caught Dad reading his love letters. According to Dad—very juicy stuff—and he still gets a kick out of the fact that he read them. But the fight got so bad their Father had to intervene, and he came down hard on Al, since he was older and should have known better. The brothers didn't speak to each other for a year. Al had no idea Dad was even on the school chess team, not until his friends told him when he came home for Dad's Bar Mitzvah. And Al never mentioned the incident with the love letters again.

Shavl — The Russians (Soviets, Communists)

Dad's Bar Mitzvah was in the spring of 1940. Like parents today, Dad's parents hired a tutor to help Dad prepare the chanting of his Haftorah, *Metzora,* from *Kings II.*

Dad's Bar Mitzvah celebration wasn't nearly as nice as Al's, who received the royal treatment when times were better. Dad did, however, receive a beautiful watch from his parents with his name engraved on it. Ultimately, that watch saved his life, but more about that later.

In six months time, Maša married Yechiel Saks, at the age of twenty-one. Like Dad's Bar Mitzvah, their wedding was a small affair. They had known each other for a few years, having met in Betar, a Zionist youth movement whose mission was to instill a love for Eretz Yisrael and to develop the skills necessary for self-defense. (Al was also a member, but Dad was too young.) Maša and Yechiel made a striking couple. Maša was with ala mailas, a Yiddish expression for having all good things a girl should have—nice face, fine figure, good head on her shoulders, well-mannered, etc. (I didn't remember ever hearing that phrase before, which surprised Dad since my grandma used to say that about me.) Then there was Yechiel, a couple of years older than Maša, always perfectly groomed and dressed in a suit and tie. Dad wouldn't go as far as to call him good-looking. But I remember a particular picture of Yechiel. Dad had a shoebox filled with old photographs, which I used to cull in search of interesting people to draw. To me, Yechiel looked like a movie star. And I still have that picture I drew of him over thirty-five years ago.

Yechiel lived with his parents in a big apartment right on Vilna Street, four or five blocks from the school Maša attended. On Shabbat afternoon he would sit on his balcony, read, and watch Maša walk by with her girlfriends. She went to a Catholic school, one of only two or three Jewish girls, and they had school on Saturday. Over fifty years later Dad called Yechiel, half a world away, to ask if he knew why his sister went to a Catholic school. Yechiel said it had something to do with a dispute between his Mother and the principal at the Hebrew Gymnasium.

After they married, Maša moved into the Saks family apartment and lived with her in-laws. Fortunately the apartment was configured in such a way that the newlyweds had their privacy. When Yechiel was out of town on business, Maša would invite Dad to sleep over. He enjoyed spending time there, and the apartment was close to his school.

Dad liked Yechiel. Whenever his Mother invited him for dinner Dad would follow him around like a puppy dog. Dad's Father, on the other hand, did not care for him, at least not for his daughter. Yechiel was not college educated. He inherited his father's clothing store when his father got ill, and to his credit, he made it an even more successful business. When the Soviets came, Yechiel bought as much leather as he could find, and he made a lot of money selling jackets and coats to the Russians, who just couldn't get enough.

Back in 1936, shortly after Al's Bar Mitzvah, Yechiel had gone to South Africa to avoid mandatory military service in the Lithuania army. He had two brothers living there. At the time there was a law stating that if a person wanted to immigrate he had to do five years, in what Yechiel referred to as "the jungle." It was more like an outpost, totally removed from Western civilization, and the native people were very primitive. Yechiel owned a general store (his brother had set him up), and these people thought nothing of relieving themselves on his floor. He returned to Shavl in 1938.

Later, when they were in the concentration camps, Dad asked Yechiel why he had come back, for he must have known trouble was brewing in Germany and across Europe. Yechiel simply said he was in love with Maša and wanted to marry her.

Shavl — The Russians (Soviets, Communists)

Typically after Shabbat, Dad went out on one of the main streets, named Telz, with his friends. He had money to buy an ice cream or go to the movies. But one particular fine summer night, Dad and his friends saw Russian soldiers, trucks and tanks, all going in the wrong direction down the street, away from the German border. The soldiers didn't look too good either; they were dirty and out of order. But the boys figured the Soviets were doing some sort of military maneuver. They watched them for hours and then went home.

Early the next morning, June 22, 1941, a neighbor knocked on their door and told them that Germany declared war on the Soviet Union. Dad's Father turned on the radio and heard the announcer confirm the dreadful news—the German army had invaded Lithuania. Dad's Mother tried to call Maša on the telephone, but there was no answer. Later that afternoon she sent Dad over on his bicycle to see if there was something wrong with their phone. They were not at home; they didn't return to Shavl until about eight o'clock that evening.

Maša and Yechiel were in Tzitevian. They used to go quite frequently on the weekends to visit Yechiel's sister and brother-in-law who had a large home there. It was the same village where Dad and his family went for summer vacation. Dad hadn't thought about them until a few years ago when he was reading a book on Lithuania, *Lita*, written in Yiddish by A. Yerushalmi, a teacher from Dad's school, and he came across a story which sounded all too familiar. It was about Yechiel's sister Shoshana Saks, her husband Josef Chvaydan, and their small child. She was a dentist and he was a doctor. When they graduated medical school in 1936, they decided to move to Tzitevian where there were no doctors; Shavl, on the other hand, had plenty of Jewish doctors.

For generations the Jews and Lithuanians of this small village had lived amicably. The farmers were poor and sometimes paid

Summer 1939 — Summer 1941

the Chvaydans for their services with chickens, eggs, butter or vegetables. The farmers would also see them for problems with their cows and horses. Shoshana and Josef developed a special friendship with a high-ranking forest-officer named Rusetzkas and a teacher named Mutzkus, and both these men spent many weekends at the Chvaydans' home enjoying their hospitality.

That Sunday the Germans invaded, Yechiel strongly urged Shoshana and Josef to return with them to Shavl immediately; they'd be safer in a big city. But Josef felt that he and his family would be safer in Tzitevian where their neighbors loved and needed them. So Yechiel and Maša returned to Shavl alone, with a driver in the Chvaydan's car.

Sadly, Josef was mistaken. Within days of the German invasion a massacre ensued, and the Jews in the countryside were among the first to be killed. Rusetzkas and Mutzkus became the leaders of the murderers, and by mid-July a second massacre took place. The Chvaydans were spared at the request of the village peasants who depended on them, but Mutzkus took their possessions in exchange for their lives.

A few days later Mutzkus came and took Shoshana and the child from the house. Shoshana adamantly refused to believe her good friend would shoot her, and she died with her child in her arms, pleading for their lives. Josef had been at the home of an extremely ill patient, and when he returned his Lithuanian neighbors told him what had happened. Josef went straight to Mutzkus' house and said—"Now you can kill me too." Mutzkus was only too happy to comply.

The Lithuanians began their pogroms during the power vacuum between the Soviet retreat and the German advance, and they proved to be the Nazis greatest collaborators. Not only did they use their fingers to point out their fellow countrymen who happened to be Jews, they used those same fingers to pull the trigger.

43

Shavl — The Russians (Soviets, Communists)

As a result, Dad's hatred for the Lithuanians was even greater than for the Nazis. The Lithuanians volunteered to work in Germany, for the Wehrmacht (the regular armed forces), and also for the Schutzstaffel (the SS), in charge of the Final Solution. Dad learned this firsthand from a neighbor who enlisted. The Lithuanians regarded the Nazis as their liberators from Communist rule and their stepping stone to autonomy, an ill-conceived notion at best. Lithuanian partisans (a misnomer if ever there was one) distinguished themselves all over Eastern Europe by killing Jews. They assisted the Nazis in murdering over ninety percent of Lithuania's Jewish population, the greatest percentage in all of Europe. It was during these first bloodbaths that Sonia, Boris Pruchno's widow, was murdered in Ponovezh.

SHAVL — THE GERMANS (NAZIS)

✣ ✣ ✣

SUMMER 1941

In a surprise attack, the Germans disregarded their Pact with the Soviet Union and overran the Baltic States in one week, with no resistance. No one thought the German blitzkrieg (lightning war) would be so successful—that the Soviets would not, or could not, put up a more impressive fight.

The first response of the young Jews of Shavl was to flee the German invasion. Dad's parents encouraged their children to run from the advancing troops for the Russian border. The Nazis and the Lithuanian partisans issued an order that if a home was vacated for a few nights, it would be confiscated; they concluded the occupant had sided with the Communists. A thousand people set out on foot and in wagons seeking refuge. Dad was fourteen-years-old at the time, and he was among them.

He went with his brother, sister and brother-in-law, although at some point Al left them and continued on with his friends. Dad, Maša and Yechiel walked all day, all night, and most of the next day. They passed Linkuva and their farm in Pamusha. They stayed on the main road together with all the other refugees.

Late in the afternoon on that first day, Yechiel picked up a rifle he found on the road. Dad asked him if he knew how to use it, not that it mattered, there was no ammunition. Yechiel responded that the Lithuanian farmers wouldn't attack them if they saw the rifle. That didn't make any sense to Dad; the farmers were just standing around watching. They were curious; they had never seen anything like this mass exodus before. Yechiel carried the rifle until daybreak and then threw it away.

After walking the country roads all night, they stopped and asked for water. (What Dad really wanted was his morning hot chocolate.) Never before had Dad known hunger or thirst. The farmers refused to give them water and advised them to move on. The farmers were afraid; the partisans were nearby and threatened punishment if they helped any Jews. Dad was born in Lithuania and felt as Lithuanian as the farmers; in seven years time he would have enlisted in the Lithuanian army. It was hard for him to understand how a fellow countryman, let alone a human being, could refuse water to another; after all, the farmers gave water to their animals.

Dad cried, but he didn't let Maša or Yechiel see him. In that hour he grew up and learned that he couldn't trust the Lithuanians. They would not likely be sympathetic to him, therefore, he shouldn't ask for anything and he wouldn't be disappointed. What's more, he knew he needed to forget his idyllic childhood and be strong, for he was going to be up against some very hard times.

At some point they left the main roads, which began filling with German soldiers shouting, "Damn Jews," and continued on auxiliary roads. By late in the afternoon they arrived in the town of Zeimelis. There they met two older Jewish women who told them the Germans had already arrived and the border had been sealed. There was no use trying to go any further.

The women, two unmarried sisters who lived with their mother, invited them in, gave them food, and offered them a place to live, not just a place to stay for the night. They were very kind and treated their guests as if they were their own children. Dad, Maša and Yechiel stayed there for three days ambivalent about whether to return to Shavl.

It was Yechiel who made the final decision. Although they would be safer in a bigger city, it was increasingly dangerous to

Shavl — The Germans (Nazis)

travel on foot, where there were Nazis and Lithuanian partisans to contend with, since it was obvious they were Jews. Using his watches, gold and money, Yechiel secured passage on farmers' wagons. Mostly the farmers wanted the watches, they couldn't tell if the gold was real, but they could see if a watch was working. The farmers also loaned them jackets to wear over their own clothing, so they wouldn't look so conspicuous. However, the most any farmer would travel was ten miles. In the end it took them two days and three different farmers to get back home.

The farmer who took them to the outskirts of Shavl had a horse that was not accustomed to automobiles, tanks or any mechanical sounds. Even though the farmer put blinders on the animal, whenever he heard these noises he would go wild, start running, and the farmer had no control over him. Once the horse went so fast the wagon overturned into a ditch and they all fell out. When they got up, Dad's wrist was swollen and he thought it was broken; he didn't feel much pain, but it looked awful.

The next day they arrived in Shavl. Dad was so happy to be back with his parents; he felt secure with them—a feeling he had taken for granted. From then on Dad understood that staying together was the most important thing, and he promised himself he would never leave his parents again. It took Al two more days to get home.

Dad's Mother took him to the doctor. His wrist was bruised and a bone was out of place, but nothing was broken. The doctor put his wrist in a cast with a sling around his neck and told him to keep it on for a month. After two weeks the swelling went down, and Dad found he could slip the cast on and off at his convenience. He wore it when he went to the store for bread. The line was very long, but the people waiting felt sorry for him, and they let him go to the front. Dad's Mother wondered how it was he came home so quickly.

Summer 1941

From the moment the Germans entered Shavl they turned the Jews into outcasts of society. Immediately there was a curfew. Shopping was restricted as the Nazis started to confiscate Jewish businesses and retail stores. For a time the Jews were allowed to shop in gentile stores, however, the Jews' food rations were set below those of the gentiles. The Nazis turned the synagogues into stables, and Lithuanian partisans and civilians went house-to-house demanding the Jews give up their gold and jewelry upon threat of death.

On more than one occasion the Lithuanians knocked on the Pruchno's door, and each time Dad's parents explained that someone else had already been there and taken everything. The Lithuanians had no accounting system; they had no way of knowing if they were being told the truth or a lie. One time they came to the house and wanted the radio. At this point a German military doctor, and the staff soldier assigned to him, stayed in the unit next door. (The people who rented from Dad's parents had fled.) So Dad's Mother marched over and explained to the doctor that the Lithuanians were trying to rob them. Their behavior enraged the Nazis; they considered the Jews' possessions German property. The doctor, a polite, middle-aged man became livid and personally came over and threatened the Lithuanians. Later on Dad's family had to give up the radio anyway.

Dad described the doctor's staff soldier as a "son of a bitch," for whenever he saw Dad he would yell at him, "Damn Jew!" Lithuanians too, young and old alike, called out, "Christ killers" and "Jews go to Palestine." It was very hard for Dad to comprehend all the hatred people felt for the Jews. Growing up Dad didn't see signs in his neighborhood like he did when he came to the United States, "No Jews or dogs allowed!" His encounters with anti-Semitism were minimal. Dad remembers his Mother asking the maid to double check that the front and back doors were locked during Easter. Once a gentile boy a few years older called Dad a "Christ killer." Dad had no idea what that meant, and not

Shavl — The Germans (Nazis)

wanting to bother his Father, he asked Yechiel. So Dad learned that the Christians blamed the Jews for killing Jesus, although it made no sense to him—if Jesus is God, how can he be killed? Dad was struck (then and now) by the fact that so many gentiles didn't even know that Jesus was Jewish. Dad thought—since when did killing a Jew become such a big deal, it surely wasn't during the pogroms in Russia and Poland?

In just two weeks the Nazis proclaimed that the Jews were not allowed to walk on the sidewalks, and that they had to wear a yellow Star of David on their clothes. At the beginning they only had to wear the Star on the front of their clothing, then a new order was issued and they had to wear it on the back as well. Dad and others put their stars on each end of a string and flopped them over their shoulders, that way they could easily be taken on and off. Later the Nazis ordered that the Star had to be sewn on permanently. These ever-increasing restrictions went on for two months—then the Jews were forced to give up their homes and move to the ghetto, formerly the slum of the city.

SHAVL — GHETTOS

✡ ✡ ✡

SUMMER 1941 — SUMMER 1944

The procedure for relocating to the ghetto varied from city to city. In Shavl, the Jews had two weeks to organize, in Kovno—three to four weeks, in Vilna—one day. Some cities, including Shavl, had two ghettos, one established after the other was filled. The Nazis told the Jews the resettlement was for their own protection and would last only for the duration of the war. The Lithuanians living in the most run down part of town now had the opportunity to trade homes with the incoming Jews.

Dad's parents debated whether or not to trade their home with a Lithuanian family. It was a very difficult decision. The ghetto was being overrun by people from the surrounding villages trying to escape the massacres by the Lithuanian partisans. The Nazis tried to pass off the shootings as aberrations committed by a few bad men. All the same, these Jews thought they'd be safer in a bigger community.

A general panic ensued to meet the German deadline for resettlement. If a place wasn't secured in the ghetto a family could be divided; a family member could be sent anywhere or could even be killed. A large number of Jews were forced to move into an area that used to house a much smaller number of gentile Lithuanians. But even more frightening to Dad's parents than the ever decreasing space in the ghetto, was their suspicion that the Lithuanians would prefer to see them dead, rather than relinquish their new found fortune of a nicely furnished home should Germany lose the war.

Summer 1941 — Summer 1944

Dad's parents looked at a few ghetto houses. They were dilapidated, the water had to be pumped, and the toilet was outside. They knew their home was worth a great deal more than any ghetto house, nevertheless, they arranged an exchange.

Dad helped his Mother bury the silver, in two metal milk containers in the chicken coop; she thought they'd be back in a few months. Still, it was heart breaking to see her give up everything. Even now Dad has a desire to go back and dig up the silver, despite the fact that our Welsh cousin, Michael Pruchnie, who visited Lithuania, informed him that a big apartment building is located on the site where his house once stood.

Just before they moved to the ghetto, Dad's Father disappeared for most of the day. Only afterwards did he tell his family he had gone to the Gauleiter, the German regional leader. His Father said that as soon as he started talking the Gauleiter asked him where he had learned to speak the German language so beautifully; he spoke a better German than most Germans. He replied that he had been educated in Konigsberg, and so the Gauleiter called in a few officers to hear him speak. Dad's Father then commented that he remembered a very different Germany, and asked the Gauleiter how a nation that produced Beethoven, Mozart, Schiller and Goethe could commit such vulgar acts against other human beings. The Gauleiter retorted that he would let him go this time—but if he ever came back again—he would never return to his family. Dad's Father left broken-hearted; the culture that had educated him had now turned against him.

In mid-August 1941, when Dad was fourteen-years-old, the Pruchnos moved to the Kavkaz ghetto. The day was sunny, so their spirits were high, and they were hopeful that the war would be over soon. Dad's Father stated, "Wait until winter comes, then the Soviets will succeed in destroying the Germans." He explained that Napoleon couldn't cope with the Russian winters and had to retreat—and the Germans would fare no better. The family made a few trips transporting some of their things in suitcases and wheelbarrows. They also hired a Jewish man with a horse and cart to help them move the bigger items. They took with them two beds, a small couch, a few chairs, blankets, pillows, pots, tablecloths, fabric, fur coats and even some books. But the majority of their possessions they left behind.

The ghetto house was crowded; Dad's family occupied one long room and a small kitchen. Dad's parents had a bed, Maša and Yechiel had a bed, and Dad and Al shared the couch. One week later Dad's Mother took in Mordechai, the Jewish farmer from Pamusha. He had left the farm after the murder of his brother, sister-in-law and niece at the hands of the Lithuanian partisans. He was very helpful to Dad's Mother. There was a wood stove, and not only did he make the fire, but he obtained the firewood, no easy task. He slept on a wooden bench in the kitchen.

Also with them, in a separate small room, was a woman with her five-year-old daughter. They were not from Shavl. The Lithuanian partisans had killed her husband during the first week of the war. The little girl looked like Shirley Temple and was quite headstrong; she was constantly asking for chocolate. Dad thought she was spoiled and couldn't understand why everybody was so taken with her.

One day a man from the Judenrat (Jewish Council), in charge of space allocation, decided that they needed to take in one more person, a Polish Jew from Warsaw, who Dad remembers as "Stanley." When the war broke out Stanley had fled to Lithuania, along with thousands of others. He was polite, had a slight stutter, and was a good master electrician. He proved to be a godsend.

So there they were, ten people forced to live in extremely cramped quarters. Keeping themselves and the household clean posed a tremendous challenge; ever present was the danger of a typhus outbreak.

Summer 1941 — Summer 1944

Attached to the ghetto house was a shack, where the previous occupants had kept their chickens; it was now filled with boxes of books, since there was no room in the house with so many people there. The books belonged to Dad's parents and some neighbors. In particular, Dad remembers a book written in Yiddish by the historian Simon Dubnow. Dad spent hours on Sundays, his only free time, standing in the shack reading about Jewish history, long after it had turned cold outside.

Dad began thinking more and more about why the Jews didn't have their own country, when Eretz Yisrael was theirs, God given according to the Bible. He asked Yechiel about it, and he replied that Ze'ev Jabotinsky (leader of Betar), David Ben-Gurion (Israel's future Prime Minister), and others, were continuing the work begun by Theodor Herzl (father of Zionism) some forty years prior, and the time would come soon. But Dad couldn't help thinking—if only they would work a little faster!

The Nazis issued orders to be implemented by the Judenrat, originally comprised of leaders of the pre-war Jewish community, which served as liaison between the Nazis and the inhabitants of the ghetto. The Judenrat was responsible for the day-to-day operations of the ghetto, like distribution of food, water, fuel, medicine and shelter—and in conjunction with the Jewish police, law and order. They were also forced to carry out the Nazi's anti-Jewish policies, such as supplying people for slave labor and deportation. Some Jews viewed the members of the Judenrat as collaborators; others viewed them as a necessary evil. To Dad, most of them were simply doing the best they could under very difficult circumstances.

Men of a certain age were forced to work outside the ghetto, work that involved all kinds of hard physical labor. Yechiel and Al had to go to work six days a week and at times on Sundays.

Dad's Father was too old; and at fourteen, Dad was considered too young, but that would soon change.

Maša asked her girlfriend from school to help her get a job working for her uncle, a priest—but the girl refused. Dad could not understand how a neighbor, who had spent so much time in their house, could become so cold-hearted. Not one of Maša's classmates asked if there was something they could do to help her or her family.

German policy was to starve the Jews in the ghetto. Bread and potatoes were the basic subsistence. The bread was black, at times stale, at other times moldy. The potatoes were often frozen. Occasionally there was flour, horsemeat, or a little fish in some state of decay. At first their former maid brought food to Dad's family—bread, potatoes, eggs, cheese and butter, and his Mother gave her clothes and fabric in exchange. The transaction took place at the ten-foot high wire fence, only a few houses away, while the guards turned their heads. But after a month it stopped—it became too dangerous for her, and for them. Notices were then posted that anyone who got too close to the fence would be arrested, and the German soldiers and Lithuanian partisans strictly enforced this policy, positioning themselves by the fence continuously.

Dad didn't know how his Mother did it, but she always cooked a tasty meal, even when they were in the ghetto. But he noticed that she was becoming too thin. When he told her she needed to eat too, she replied that she had gotten enough to eat by tasting the food as she prepared it.

Dad started "leaving" the ghetto by way of the bordering cemetery to obtain the extra food they needed to survive. His Mother didn't want him to go into the city and trade with the Lithuanians; it was too dangerous. But Dad told her, "It's nothing—it's like a game." He didn't want her to worry. Dad went because he felt it was the right thing to do. He was younger and it was easier for him to hop over the cemetery wall, and truth be told, he liked being the hero. Dad used to raise himself up on the wall to see where the guards were stationed; when they went in the opposite direction, Dad hopped over the wall, raced across the field to the street, and mixed with the Lithuanians. There he traded away the family's valuables for life's necessities.

A few times Dad heard, "Hey, Jew boy, you should be in the ghetto, I should report you to the Germans." The Nazis had hung up notices stating that a person could obtain five pounds of sugar, salt or cigarettes for turning in a Jew.

Getting back into the ghetto was a bit harder since Dad's hands were full. Again he watched for the guards; then he took his bag of food, threw it over the wall, and jumped after it. Dad had no fear—at least that's what he says now. But being caught for smuggling food into the ghetto carried a penalty—imprisonment. Still, it was an acceptable risk, because to do nothing meant death.

After a few weeks in the ghetto, Dad started working on the outside and he stopped hopping the cemetery wall. He was then able to trade with the Lithuanians at work.

One Sunday morning in September, Dad was sitting around talking with a boy his age named Isaac, whom he met in the ghetto. Isaac was a religious kid, who wore a yarmulke (skull cap), and went to a school called Yavneh. They talked about their lives under normal conditions, and how by this time of the year they would have already returned to school. They talked about their concerns for the future as well.

As they spoke, a Jewish policeman ran by yelling that the Lithuanian partisans needed seventy men immediately to work outside the ghetto for a few days, and if a crew was not assembled within half an hour, they would come take men at random. The policeman suggested that Dad and Isaac volunteer, otherwise their fathers could be taken. The boys agreed; they thought to spare their fathers since the work would be easier for them, but first they wanted to tell their parents. However, the policeman knew that if they went "home" their parents would never allow them to go, so he told them not to worry, that he would inform their parents.

It didn't take long and the men were all assembled, young and old, including Mordechai and a few others Dad knew. They were taken to the railway station where they took a very slow moving train to a place near Pamusha, close to the Pruchno's and Mordechai's farms. Once there, they were put in a barn and told they could write "home" to say they arrived safely. They were given small pieces of paper, pencils, and five minutes. Dad wrote his name and street, he couldn't remember the number, he wrote that he was fine and that Mordechai was with him.

In the evening they were given soup made with pig fat, which they did not eat, and a slice of black bread. When it was time to sleep, there were no blankets or pillows, only straw. They took off their shoes, put them behind their heads, and slept in their clothes. Dad slept between his friend and Mordechai, who kindly covered Dad with his jacket.

In the morning they were woken up and given some tea and black bread. Then they were counted. But the Lithuanian partisans were having a hard time getting the tally right. A member of their group, an engineer, suggested that he be the group's spokesman and offered to help with the count. The partisans agreed, and soon they were ready to go to work laying railroad tracks.

The city government never had the finances to complete the railroad tracks into town, but now it had a free labor force. The Lithuanian foreman and guards, who were acclimated to this type of work, instructed their new "recruits." However, it was very physically demanding labor and many of the Jews were not accustomed to it. Even though their spokesman made certain the strong worked alongside the weak, they still were not able to do the work according to the Lithuanians' standards, and they were not meeting the daily quotas. As a result, the partisans were getting angry.

When the gentile farmers saw Mordechai, their former neighbor, they spoke with him for a short while. The next day they brought him a bag filled with food—bread, butter, cheese, ham, eggs and milk. Later in the evening when they all sat down, Mordechai placed the whole bag in front of Dad and told him to eat whatever he wanted. Dad was overwhelmed with his compassion and generosity. He didn't know what to do; it was Mordechai's food, yet he couldn't very well start eating it in front of Isaac. Dad quietly asked him if he could give some of the food to his friend. Mordechai responded that Dad should consider the food his own, and that they would get more. So Dad shared the food, they didn't eat the ham, and the next day they did indeed receive more. Thanks to those bags of food, their spirits remained high, and they didn't even bother with the meager meals provided by the partisans.

At night they were locked up, and because they were not allowed to go outside to relieve themselves, a pail was placed in the barn. There were no bathroom facilities anyway. During the day they relieved themselves in the woods and wiped with leaves. After a while they had to be careful where they stepped. They had no change of clothing and the straw beds were itching them—it was awful.

On Saturday nights the Lithuanian partisans left and got drunk. The Jews were afraid that when they returned they would set the barn on fire; they had heard rumors to that effect. On Sundays the door was opened later than usual with the partisans demanding watches and gold, but the Jews didn't have anything to give. And again the partisans were furious with them.

A few days became three weeks and still they received no

news from the ghetto regarding their status. Then their circumstances changed. There was an airfield near Shavl and the Germans decided to enlarge it. They needed five hundred men and women from the ghetto for this project. The Judenrat informed the Germans that seventy good workers had already been taken out of the ghetto to work for the Lithuanian partisans. The Germans immediately commandeered those workers for the airfield. A German guard and a member of the Judenrat were sent to retrieve them. Working at the airfield was a much better arrangement. Even though it was a one-hour walk each way, Dad and his co-workers could now go "home" to the ghetto in the evenings.

Although his family had received Dad's note, his parents gave him a good scolding upon his return. He should never volunteer! He was too young to make those kinds of decisions for himself! The sad reality was they never really knew when an order was issued—were they actually going to work or were they going to be shot?

The Nazis, with the help of the Lithuanian partisans, often conducted "Aktions" or "Selections," where specific groups of people, such as children, were targeted for deportation and eventual murder. Dad knew some of the families whose children were abducted. The Jews were told the children would be sent to a sanatorium where they would receive better care than possible in the ghetto. The Judenrat was suspicious; children belonged with their mothers, and a member named Aharon Katz voiced their fears. A Nazi officer replied that since he was challenging their honor, he would accompany the children. Needless to say, no one from the Children's Aktion was ever seen or heard from again.

Many times the Nazis searched the ghetto for people without work certificates. Most of the people they found were older, and they were rounded up and taken away. Only one member of a

Summer 1941 — Summer 1944

family was allowed to stay in the ghetto without such a document, and that edict could be rescinded at any time. Typically it was the woman of the household who did not have a certificate, but Dad's Father did not have one either. On those mornings when the inhabitants of the ghetto sensed something was amiss, Dad's Father would accompany his sons and "volunteer" for work that day. While the men were at work, the houses were searched. A few times Dad's Mother and the woman with her "Shirley Temple" daughter hid in the cellar—and once the little girl would not stop crying. Fortunately, the Nazis never did find the cellar; the access panel was in the floor, covered by a carpet, table and chairs.

Dad began work on the airfield under the German company, Organisation Todt, during the fall of 1941. Hitler himself hand picked Fritz Todt, a civil engineer, to construct the Autobahn in 1933, which became the envy of the industrialized world. It also enabled Hitler to move his troops faster and in greater numbers than ever before in history.

In addition to the airfield expansion, they built large underground furnaces to heat airplane engines, which couldn't start in the cold. Normally the pilot started the engine with only the ignition, however, in freezing temperatures a crank at the front of the plane had to be turned with a special wrench as well, and at times Dad was assigned this task. Dad only pretended to turn the crank, moving his body and scrunching his face with the supposed effort. There was no way Dad was going to help the Nazis get off the ground.

Besides the Jews, there were many Russian prisoners at the airfield as well. In fact, the Nazis were just as cruel, if not more so, to them. A young German soldier would throw a slice of bread into the air, and a group of starving Russian prisoners would all try to catch it, while his buddies laughed. Some of the Russians

Shavl — Ghettos

would fall and not be able to get up. Then another German soldier would jump on the fallen prisoner's chest until his last breath was squeezed out of him, and once again they laughed. It was like some grotesque sporting event. It was so terrible that when Dad imagined his vengeance against the Nazis, it was on behalf of those Russians as well.

One hot summer day in 1942, a group of Lithuanian partisans removed about eighty men from the ghetto, Dad and Al included. The men were ordered to move some hefty pieces of lumber from one place to another, lumber so heavy it took a dozen men to move a single piece. When the job was complete, they did not receive the promised food and water. Instead they were ordered to move it all back again. The men, mostly young, their tempers rising, flatly refused to comply with this exercise in futility. The partisans threatened to shoot them if they didn't start moving. A stalemate ensued during which a Jewish policeman ran back to the ghetto for help. Hurriedly, a member of the Judenrat arrived and bribed the Lithuanians with watches and money; humbly promising it would never happen again.

Stanley, the final member to join their household, worked as an electrician in a German military hospital, and he took on Yechiel as his assistant. (The men had become friendly; they both smoked and Yechiel gave him cigarettes.) Yechiel caught on quickly and the Germans had no idea he wasn't also an experienced electrician. Not only did Yechiel learn a trade, he received a certificate that stated he worked outside the ghetto. After a while Stanley took on Al as a helper, and then Dad too, at fifteen years of age. Stanley gave them their assignments and instructed them on "job security"—work diligently only when the German bosses could see them work—otherwise they should take their time.

Dad's job was to chisel holes in the walls to run electrical cable for medical equipment. One day he had to climb a ladder up to the second floor. At the top Dad looked through the window and saw German soldiers bandaged up like Egyptian mummies, with only their eyes showing. Dad enjoyed this sight so much he took his sweet time chiseling the hole. One soldier came up to the window, he could easily see the Star of David on Dad's clothing, and he started yelling, "Damn Jew, look at all the trouble you cause!" The soldier was outraged and tried to open the window, but couldn't. Dad was sure his intention was to push the ladder over. Still, Dad didn't miss an opportunity to see the wounded soldiers; it gave him hope that the war would be over soon.

It was that cold winter of 1942-43 that the Germans were defeated at Stalingrad, in what many considered the turning point of the war. Dad's Father had been correct, only it happened a winter later than hoped.

In the meantime, the work at the hospital was good, it was mostly inside, and for Dad and Al it lasted through the winter. Yechiel, however, had a steady job maintaining the building. More importantly, working outside the ghetto provided the Jews the opportunity they so desperately needed—to smuggle food into the ghetto. If they saw anything unusual on their return, such as different guards, or more of them, they would simply drop their food before they got too close to the gate. Now the penalty for smuggling food was death!

In late spring of 1943, Betzalel Mazovietski was caught returning to the ghetto with meat and cigarettes. The Nazis suspected the Jews of bringing in food from the outside because they weren't dying off fast enough based upon the rations they were given. Mazovietski was beaten and jailed, then sentenced to hang. The inhabitants of both ghettos were ordered to witness his execution at Jewish hands. According to Yerushalmi's account in *Lita*, the

Shavl — Ghettos

Judenrat had tried in vain to save his life, but the best they could do was to arrest his wife and parents, so they would not have to be present at his hanging. Mazovietski was courageous, preferring to die rather than divulge the name of his Lithuanian contact and jeopardize the meager lifeline to the ghetto. Before he took his last breath he requested that his coat be removed because it did not belong to him and that his boots be given to his brother. Then he forgave the hangman and asked forgiveness from his fellow Jews.

Another time the Judenrat was ordered to compile a list of fifty names, innocent people who were to be shot for the crime of smuggling food. The Nazis employed the concept of collective responsibility to discourage any unwanted behaviors. After much deliberation, the Judenrat put themselves and the Jewish police on the list. In the end they were ransomed by the Jewish community for twenty thousand Reichsmarks. Unfortunately, things of this nature happened all too often.

As previously mentioned, Shavl had two ghettos (about a twenty-minute walk between them), and in the beginning the Pruchnos lived in Kavkaz ghetto. When two ghettos were no longer necessary, because too many Jews had been deported and/or murdered, Kavkaz, the larger of the two, was shut down, and within a couple of days they were forced to move to Trako ghetto. Their old friend Mordechai remained in Kavkaz, and Dad never saw him again.

In Trako they lived in a large room, on the second floor of a house, and the conditions were even worse than at Kavkaz. Maša and Yechiel shared a bed, while Dad and Al shared a couch. Dad's Father slept on a couch and his Mother slept on two chairs pushed together. Everybody worked outside the house except Dad's Mother. His Father only worked sometimes; other times he stood in line for the family's rations, which by the time it was his turn, were not necessarily available. This precarious existence was particularly hard on him. Besides the difficulties in procuring food, there were the difficulties in obtaining wood for cooking and warmth. They were only given a one or two day supply of wood for an entire month. So during the summer they would already be thinking about where to obtain wood for the winter. Dad's Mother made sure a fire was going when everyone returned from work so they could dry themselves and their clothing. They were in the Kavkaz and Trako ghettos from August 1941 to November 1943.

From then until July 1944, they stayed in the A.B.A., or the Armee-Bekleidungs-Amt (Army Clothing Depot). Not that they had a choice, but Dad's parents thought it would be safer if they worked directly for the Germans; they trusted the Lithuanians that much less. The man in charge was named Oigul, and he was sympathetic toward the Jews. According to Dad it was the best camp they had been in to date. The prisoners stayed in a newly erected barracks that was no more than a big room filled with bunks, but it was clean. For privacy they hung sheets between the families. Dad referred to it as a glorified concentration camp, without the killing. The truth was, Dad felt safer there, he didn't feel like they would be taken out and shot at any moment.

A Polish Jew from Krakow came to the A.B.A. His name was Rosen, and he was a professional welder and toolmaker. One day the Nazis inquired after someone with his particular skills, and he volunteered. Under German supervision he was put in charge of building a military laundering facility for the washing and disinfecting of German uniforms from the Russian front. Rosen knew Dad vaguely from Al, and as luck would have it, he asked Dad to become his helper. The job involved mostly manual labor, such as cutting and bending pipes, but it kept Dad inside during the cold winter months of 1943-44, so he gladly accepted the offer.

It was very primitive work. In order to bend a pipe, Dad had to fill the pipe with sand, block the ends with pieces of wood, heat the place to be bent, and then bend the pipe by hand. If it cracked, as it sometimes did, Rosen would then have to weld the crack. But Dad did not mind the work, and after a while Rosen had at least five other helpers.

While under construction the "laundromat" was partially operational. Trainloads of uniforms would arrive anytime, day or night, and they would have to be unloaded immediately for the train to stay on schedule. Sometimes the clothing was in good shape, but other times it was a bloody mess. The facility was fully operational for only about a month. As the Soviets advanced into the Baltic States, the Germans dismantled it and shipped all the machinery back to Germany.

While working at the laundromat, Dad became very close friends with a man named Yitzchak Lasynski, a toolmaker, about eight years older than Dad who was then sixteen. He was married to a woman named Malka, and they had one child, two-years-old, who they gave to a Lithuanian family to keep safe. But they had a hard time, for they had no valuables to trade for the little boy's upkeep.

To make a little money, Yitzchak acted as middleman between the Jews and Lithuanians. Dad's Mother, among others, gave him their valuables to trade for life's necessities. Dad helped him as well, as he phrased it, "by stealing." While at work Dad set aside some of the officer's uniforms; the pants had leather seats, and Yitzchak cut out this valuable commodity.

Yitzchak then donned a German sergeant's uniform, walked to the gate, saluted "Heil Hitler" to the Lithuanian guards, and into the city he went, to see his son and pay the family. He had to be careful not to run into any German military personnel, who

Summer 1941 — Summer 1944

might ask to see his papers and inquire after his business. But Yitzchak could walk around the city with relative ease because he didn't "look Jewish."

Dad used to tease him, "Are you sure you're Jewish?" When Dad first met Yitzchak he thought he was a spy; he was blond and couldn't speak Yiddish. It wasn't until Dad met his wife that he was convinced Yitzchak was O.K.

Yitzchak found getting back into camp, however, wasn't as easy as getting out. It was late at night, around ten or eleven o'clock, and there was no reason for a sergeant to be returning at that late hour. Instead of bluffing his way through the gate, Yitzchak had to crawl under the fence. Dad watched for him and they developed signals as to when it was safe for him to proceed.

Dad asked him, "Why not be a captain, or a higher ranking officer?" Yitzchak explained that it would be too risky, high ranking officers never went anywhere alone. A sergeant was good enough, and it kept him out of trouble. Now I understand why Dad so thoroughly enjoyed the TV show *Hogan's Heroes*—it reminded him of Yitzchak's exploits.

One day Yitzchak suggested that they watch for handguns and hand grenades when the soldiers clothing arrived for laundering. Yitzchak was not at work the day Dad found four grenades. Dad couldn't pass up the opportunity, and he hid them in a safe place in the work camp, in some corner with clothes thrown over them. (Sometimes the best hiding place is right out in the open.) That evening Dad told Yitzchak about his find, and they agreed to keep the secret to themselves.

Since they had access to tools, Yitzchak decided to take apart one of the grenades to see how it worked. Dad wasn't exactly thrilled with the idea; he had seen the Germans practicing with them and saw how powerful they were. But to prove he wasn't a coward he stood by Yitzchak, on the lookout for a surprise visit. Besides, they had a deal—Yitzchak promised that when he escaped he'd take Dad with him. Thankfully the experiment proved uneventful.

Yitzchak kept two grenades and Dad kept one. They brought their grenades into the A.B.A., since there was always the possibility that they'd be taken elsewhere to work. It was a half hour walk from the work camp to the A.B.A., and they were often searched at the gate when they returned. The Nazis would have hanged Dad and shot a hundred people or more, including Dad's family, had they found the grenade on him. So Dad acquired a fresh loaf of bread from a Lithuanian, from which he removed the inside and inserted the grenade; then he brought it into camp. This also carried some risk, but Dad had figured out which guards were more lenient than others. Once inside the camp, Dad wrapped the grenade in linen and hid it in the roof gutter at the barracks.

Near the end of winter, February 1944, Dad's Father got very sick with kidney problems, and they had to put him in the Trako ghetto hospital. He was there about six weeks and Dad's Mother spent a lot of time with him; sometimes Dad wouldn't see her for an entire week. His doctor was one of their family's physicians before the war, Dr. Paysachovitz; he was also the head of the ghetto hospital. It was very hard on Dad's Mother, and they were hoping his Father would be released soon.

One day Dad's Father asked to see him. Dad obtained permission from one of the Jewish administrators of the A.B.A., who had been Dad's teacher at the Hebrew Gymnasium, an honest man by the name of Baruch Broyde. Dad's Mother had to stay behind; only one person per family was allowed to visit the hospital at a time. A Lithuanian guard and Jewish policeman escorted Dad, along with other Jewish prisoners, from the work camp to the ghetto hospital. It was over an hour walk.

When Dad walked into the hospital it was as though he had been physically struck. It was indescribably awful. It was overcrowded with ten people in a room, it was smelly and dirty, and ants were crawling everywhere. At times the hospital was so overcrowded that Jews were taken out and shot, just to make more room.

Dad barely recognized his Father. He wished his Mother had prepared him. He felt tears running down his face and turned his head so his Father wouldn't see him cry. Dad tried to make his Father more comfortable by repositioning his pillow, and he asked if there was anything he could get for him. His Father wanted juice; his mouth was dry. Dad's Mother had instructed him that if there was anything his Father needed he should go to their old neighbor and family friend who lived nearby. Dad went straightaway and the woman promised she would prepare some juice. In the meantime, Dad went to see Dr. Paysachovitz.

The doctor told Dad his Father was very sick, and in normal times, with the proper medication, he would be able to cure him. As it was, there was nothing he could do for him. Dad was angry at the doctor, angry at the world, and he yelled, "If you were the captain of a ship, you wouldn't give up the ship just because there was a storm at sea! Don't give up on him! Help him!"

Dad then returned for the juice, thanked the neighbor, and quickly ran back to the hospital. Dad naively gave the juice to his Father as though it were a magic tonic. Dad asked the nurse if he could stay with his Father overnight, and she found him a chair. As Dad sat down his Father bent toward him and said, "What will happen to you? You are so young. Be honest. Someone will appreciate your honesty." Then he fell asleep, and Dad did too.

By morning he was dead. It was a terrible shock to Dad. Chaim Yitzchak Pruchno was buried that day in a cemetery near Kavkaz ghetto. Only Dad, his Mother, and a few neighbors who lived nearby were present. That evening, April 7, 1944, was Erev Pesach. Dad never forgot the last words his Father's spoke, "Be honest"—they have been a guiding light throughout his life.

Shavl — Ghettos

At the end of June, when the prisoners returned from work, they saw more guards than usual and knew something was underfoot. On Monday morning everyone had to leave the barracks to hear an announcement by Erich Gidansky, the Jewish superintendent of the work camp. He was from Memel on the Baltic Sea, young, good looking, well mannered, and fluent in German. He told them they were going to be shipped to Germany, and that they would be working for the same Germans under the same conditions—at least that's what the Germans had told him.

After his speech they returned to the barracks. A while later a number of the men got together, without the Judenrat knowing, to discuss the possibility of breaking out of the A.B.A. and running to Linkaytchiay Forest, which was close enough to camp that it was worth considering. The men were re-evaluating their idea of what constituted the greater danger. Was it the possibility of running into Lithuanian partisans, or the certainty of being deported to the unknown? The younger people could run, and they might make it, but there were those who could not run. What if a husband and wife were running and one of them got shot, would one leave the other? Would a son leave his mother? Of course, there were the hot heads who were not responsible for anybody. This discussion continued on until it was time to disperse; they also didn't want to draw the attention of the German guards.

The next few days were not "normal" as people left and went into hiding. Dad spoke with Yitzchak the day before he and Malka escaped. They had little choice; their son was being shuffled around because they could not afford his upkeep. Dad reminded Yitzchak of their deal—to take him with when they escaped—Dad thought they would fight the Nazis together. But Yitzchak told Dad his place was with his Mother. I think Yitzchak didn't even consider taking Dad along because he thought it was unlikely they would survive with the liability of their small child.

Summer 1941 — Summer 1944

As they learned in the upcoming days, many people didn't make it. They were shot by the Lithuanian partisans. However, Yitzchak and his family did, and he kept his grenades with him until the end of the war.

It wasn't until the end of 1979, when my Mom and Dad were in Israel for the first time, that Dad found out the Lasynskis had survived. And it wasn't until the early 1990s before they had their long overdue reunion.

STUTTHOF

✣ ✣ ✣

SUMMER 1944

Under heavy guard they returned to Trako ghetto from the A.B.A. Dad took his grenade with him the same way as before. Others were transferred to the ghetto as well, including several hundred people who worked at the German airfield, and about three thousand Jews from the area surrounding Ponovezh. The ghetto was getting very crowded, even though the transports to Germany had already begun.

Dad and his family were in the ghetto for two days and were among the last to leave, along with others from the A.B.A. They were scared. They didn't know exactly where they were going, only that they were going to Germany. They each took the one permitted suitcase, all the bread they had, and some bottles filled with water. Dad's Mother also took a frying pan and a small pot in the hopes she could use them. Dad left his grenade in the ghetto.

Late in the afternoon they were pushed into boxcars, approximately eighty Jews per car. They barely had room to sit down, let alone stretch out their legs. A pail was placed in the car for community use. They put it in a corner so people could have some privacy. It didn't take long before the pail was full. They realized they should use it only for emergencies and they should hold their bowels. The smell was unbearable, especially during the day.

Dad's Mother had some jewelry and gave each of them a piece. Dad also had his cherished Bar Mitzvah watch and declared to

73

his Mother, "Nobody will take my watch from me, not if I want to survive the war." He took the band off and tucked the watch into the earflaps of his cap. Dad's Mother urged them to stay together; they could never know when one of them would need the other's help. Dad and his siblings gave her their word they would.

Occasionally their train slowed as it passed a hospital train stopped on the adjacent tracks. Right away the SS came out to make sure nobody saw the wounded soldiers. However, the Jews saw them, just barely, through the cracks in the boxcar, and the sight of bandaged soldiers lifted their spirits. Other times their train stopped for hours to let military trains pass.

Even without reading the village signs they knew when they were getting closer to Germany. The farmhouses were in better condition and the roads were more advanced than back at home. Their morale was boosted just getting away from the murderous Lithuanians. They thought life would be better in Germany. After all, the strong could work. Why else would they be taken hundreds of miles if not to work for the German war effort? If the Nazis' intention was to kill them, they could have done so back in Lithuania. The Jews had heard rumors about extermination camps—but no one believed it—it was just too monstrous to comprehend.

Extermination camps were stationary gassing facilities, built in Poland for the sole purpose of annihilating Jews with the efficiency and precision of a factory assembly line. The first one, Chelmno, was opened at the end of 1941, with Auschwitz-Birkenau being the most notorious. Concentration camps, on the other hand, were built for the incarceration and forced labor of any enemy of the Nazi regime, including gypsies, homosexuals, and political and religious opponents. The death rate in these camps due to starvation, disease, exposure and exhaustion was very high. The first such camp, opened in 1933, was Dachau.

Summer 1944

As the train moved on, Dad was daydreaming about his future after the war. At seventeen years of age, he had lost his Father and three years of schooling. Who would support them? Who would pay for schooling? Would they ever go back to Shavl? Would they need to sell their house? Where would they live?

When the train stopped, the sign said Stutthof. They were in Germany, near the Baltic Sea, about twenty miles east of the Free City of Danzig (Gdansk), in what should have been Poland, and three miles from Stutthof concentration camp.

Their boxcar stopped around a curve, so they were able to see the locomotives being changed, from civilian to SS, and some of the adults sensed something was amiss. As they proceeded closer to camp they saw barbed and electrified wires, watchtowers, and people walking around in striped uniforms. This place didn't look like anything they were familiar with; there were no factories to work in. It took two days of repeated stopping and starting, which felt like forever, but they finally arrived—although some Jews had died along the way.

When the Nazis opened the doors, the Jews were greeted with the following order, "Give us your gold and other valuables, you will not need them anymore!" They were ordered out of the boxcar, which was difficult for the older people since it was so high off the ground, but the younger ones gave them a hand. They were instructed to leave their suitcases and other belongings by the train. The Nazis forbade them from speaking to each other. Immediately the men and women were separated. It would be the last time Dad saw his Mother and sister, although he did not realize it at the time.

The men had to stand in lines and start walking; no talking was permitted. They walked quite a distance, escorted by German guards with dogs. When they came to an open place, a tall, young, SS officer, beautifully dressed in a nice uniform with

Stutthof

shiny boots, issued orders with a stick. Some men were directed to the right and others to the left. They didn't know what it meant. Dad was glad when he got to go the same direction as his brother and brother-in-law. In total they numbered a few hundred prisoners, and they were ordered to sit on the ground for some hours. The Nazis announced that anyone who stood up without permission would be shot; anyone caught with jewelry would also be shot. The Nazis thought people would start handing over their valuables, but nobody did. Dad took the gold chain his Mother had given him out of his pocket and buried it in the sand.

They looked around and saw buildings with black smoke coming out of their chimneys, and they became anxious when the German kapos yelled at them, "The only way you're getting out of here is through the chimneys!" German kapos were ex-convicts, robbers and murderers, identified by the different colored triangles on their uniforms, and they were in charge of the daily routines and rules; under them were the Jewish kapos. Dad and those around him nervously waited in line to enter one of these buildings. Then they saw prisoners, who were a good distance in front of them in line, running out of another building—naked. They were given striped pants and shirts. Why would they be given clothes if the Nazis intended to kill them? That reasoning calmed them.

The German kapos pushed and beat them with rubber sticks, ordered them to get undressed in a hurry, and shoved them into a special room. Sometime during the process Dad got separated from Al and Yechiel. The kapos cut their hair short and shaved their body hair. Dad was nervous as one kapo wielded a knife near his private parts. The kapos sat them on special chairs with their legs spread apart, to make sure they didn't have any jewelry hidden up their rectums. They were then sprayed with delousing solution and ushered into a washroom for a cold shower. Afterward they were rushed outside naked, where they were given

Summer 1944

striped uniforms with no regard for size, and then rushed to a pile of civilian shoes and caps, which originally belonged to each of them, but now they had to quickly take at random. Dad grabbed some boots and tried to put them on, but they were too small. So he ran back to exchange them, but was struck by a kapo because that was not permitted. Nevertheless, he grabbed another pair of shoes and a cap. Then Dad found Al and Yechiel.

When they were finally all lined up, Dad noticed the man in front of him was wearing his cap; he could see it bulging out a little where he had hidden his watch. He asked Yechiel how to go about getting it back. Yechiel advised Dad to ask the man to trade caps because he had photos of his parents hidden inside it. The man exchanged caps without a question. As Dad put on the cap, he felt the earflap; his watch was still there, and his hopes intact.

By the time the procedure was complete, it was dusk. They were marched to the open assembly place and told to sit down with their hands up in the air. After approximately half an hour they were told to put their hands down. If they had to go to the bathroom, they had to raise their hand and get permission; only about one in five were granted that luxury. Again, anyone who stood up without permission would be shot. They were not given any food or water that entire day. They spent the night in the open field hoping for a miracle. At least it was summer and it didn't rain.

The next morning the Nazis announced that they needed workers for a labor camp. The prisoners desperately wanted to get on the waiting trucks, and they encouraged Erich Gidansky, the superintendent, to report to the Germans that they were ready for work—anything to get away from this dreadful place. Gidansky got slapped in the face and told to speak only when told to speak.

Stutthof

They were standing in lines, six per line, with Al and Yechiel in front of Dad. A kapo was counting men for the trucks and stopped right on Dad's row. Dad panicked, he was going to be left behind! He could hear his Mother's voice saying, "Stay together"—he had promised her. So as the truck started to drive away with Al and Yechiel, Dad instinctively ran after it and clambered on board. The guards were yelling for the truck to stop, but the driver didn't hear and continued on. Dad was incredibly lucky; he could have been shot in the back! And all Yechiel could say was, "I told you to stay with us."

The prisoners were brought to a railroad station and again put into boxcars. At some point planes started dropping bombs around them, and the train stopped. The sirens sounded, and the German guards slid open the boxcar doors yelling for the prisoners to get out, while they ran and hid in the forest. As the prisoners began making their way out of the cars, they thought—let the Allies bring it on. There was nowhere for them to escape in their striped uniforms, but they were willing to sacrifice themselves to see the Nazis killed. At the very least, it felt good to see the enemy running in fear. Then the strike ended, almost as soon as it had begun, and with another blare of the siren they were forced back into the boxcars.

The train continued on unharmed. They didn't know where they were going, only that they were glad to have left Stutthof behind. Dad lost track of how many days they were on the train, and how many stops they made, as they traveled all the way across Germany to a place near Munich called Dachau, a name that meant nothing to Dad at the time.

DACHAU

✶ ✶ ✶

SUMMER 1944 — SPRING 1945

It was a sunny day when they arrived at Dachau in July 1944, and the camp looked even more menacing than Stutthof. They marched through a gate crowned with the words "Arbeit Macht Frei"—Work Makes Freedom. There they stood before a row of tables, approximately ten feet away. Al was on Dad's right, and as he approached a table, Dad approached the next one. Behind these tables sat the German kapos who very neatly wrote down their information in big ledgers with lined paper. When Dad told the kapo, "Shmuel Pruchno—Shavl, Lithuania—April 1, 1927," the kapo made a show of checking his ledger and responded, "That man is dead." Dad didn't know whether the kapo was playing games with him or not, all he knew was that it would have been far easier to have Dad shot than to modify his beautiful ledger. Dad quickly picked another date at random, "January 6, 1927." The kapo then issued Dad his number—84782. Unlike the procedure at other concentration camps, these numbers were not tattooed on their arms; they were worn on their clothing.

Dad has always celebrated this new "birthday." In fact, it's the birth date he used on his citizenship papers. For the longest time I didn't even know his true birth date. When Unc would come over to our house and wish Dad a "Happy Birthday" on April Fools Day, I thought it was a private joke.

Summer 1944 — Spring 1945

That first day at Dachau they received a bowl of watery soup with a slice of bread; that night they stayed in barracks with bunk beds covered in straw. The next morning Dad's group, over two thousand men, with German guards all around, were marched to a railroad station where they went for a short ride in an open rail car. Then they walked for a few hours, becoming increasingly hungry and thirsty. Finally the guards let them rest in a shallow valley. While they rested they saw a few airplanes coming toward them, and for a moment they thought they were going to be strafed. Then they saw the emblem of concentric circles on the wings and knew these were not German planes. The British planes circled around them once and left. No German planes challenged them; their anti-aircraft guns fired only a few feeble shots. It was a great boost for the prisoners' morale.

They resumed their march for another few hours until they reached their destination—Dachau satellite camp #2. There they saw barbed and electrified wires, watchtowers, and guards with machine guns. The Jews from Shavl tried to stick together as they were placed into barracks of about a hundred men each. The tops of the barracks were covered with dirt and grass. There was a door at one end and only a small window at the other end. It was like walking into the side of a hill, and from the sky the barracks could not be seen.

There was a small steel stove in the center and Dad, Al and Yechiel were fortunate to get bunks close to it. They took the lower bunks, even though they couldn't sit up straight due to the bunks above. To get in they had to slide in from the front. The bunks were wood platforms, covered in straw that was never changed. Since they always slept in the same bunk, they came to know their neighbors. Opposite them were Jews from Greece, and nearby there were Lithuanian, Polish and Hungarian Jews.

That evening they received their first "meal" in camp. It consisted of scant amounts of bread, margarine, cheese and soup.

Dachau

Feivel Krotenberg was the man in Dad's section elected to slice the loaves of bread into equal pieces.

At nine o'clock the two bare light bulbs were turned off and no talking was permitted. Dad slept between Al and Yechiel. They had each received one blanket, which Dad and Al shared. They placed one blanket underneath them to somewhat protect them from the itchy straw, and the other they used to cover themselves. They removed their shirts and rolled them up to use as pillows, and put their shoes behind their heads so no one would steal them. They were so exhausted they quickly fell asleep.

At four-thirty in the morning the lights went on and a German kapo yelled at them to get up—it was time for washing and coffee. The facilities were primitive and not large enough to accommodate so many people. When they walked into the washroom they saw a long pipe with holes, and water dripping from it; there were neither bars of soap nor towels. Nearby was the latrine where they had to carefully squat to relieve themselves so as not to fall in, and the stench was dreadful. There was nothing to wipe with; they would use leaves or pieces of cement bags when they could find them.

The coffee situation was no better. They had to walk in line at a fast pace as a German kapo poured the coffee from a big container. Most of the coffee spilled on the ground, because another German kapo stood there hitting the prisoners with a rubber stick should they actually stop and give the coffee a chance of making it into their metal cups. There was only so much time for coffee and so many people to serve. Dad, Al and Yechiel rarely went for coffee after that, it wasn't worth the risk of getting hit. The kapo didn't care what body part he hit; a prisoner could receive a blow to his head. It was absurd. It was better to wait in the barracks and forego the washing and the coffee.

Summer 1944 — Spring 1945

Everything was new to them and everything had to be done at a fast pace. That first morning, after washing and coffee, they started to return to the barracks, but the kapos hit them and pushed them to the appelplatz (the place for roll call). There they stood by block number, while the block kapo counted them to be sure all were present. Then he reported to a German kapo (in charge of five blocks), who reported to a German officer, who then reported to the Commandant. Roll call occurred in the morning before leaving for work and in the evening upon returning, and if the count was not right it could take hours. The Nazis were always afraid that a prisoner had escaped. Roll call occurred regardless of the weather. The prisoners, in their striped uniforms, had to stand outside in rain or snow, in order and not moving. It wasn't just the cold of winter that was difficult, but summer's sweltering heat too.

Once during roll call Dad had to go to the latrine. He had diarrhea and couldn't afford to dirty his pants; he wouldn't get another pair. He didn't have time to ask for permission, besides, his request could have been denied. He was standing close to the latrine, so he quickly slipped out of line, did his business, and slipped back in. Dad didn't go unnoticed; a Jewish kapo started yelling at him and hitting him. Dad knew the kapo had to do his job, or he would get beaten himself, but still Dad asked why he was hitting him so hard. The kapo responded that better he should hit him than a German, who would undoubtedly do it much harder. But Dad couldn't keep his mouth shut and told him that he hoped he'd meet up with him after the war. The Jewish kapo didn't like Dad's remark and called for assistance from a German kapo. The German beat Dad over his head with a big stick, as Dad tried to protect himself with his hands.

Another opportunity for getting hit involved a "game" the German kapos enjoyed. They would yell, "caps up, caps down," and the prisoners had to perform in a synchronized manner or get hit. Roll call was one of the cruelest experiences of the concentration camp.

Once roll call was completed they walked for approximately one hour, sometimes longer, to their work assignment—the Ringeltaube project. The main work involved the building of three semi-subterraneous bombproof bunkers in the Landsberg area, code named Walnut II, Vineyard II and Diana II. The purpose of these bunkers was to camouflage the manufacture of the newest Messerschmitt airplanes, so production could proceed uninterrupted by Allied bombings. The bunkers were so enormous that entire freight trains could pull into them and look like little more than toys. The first plans were over ambitious, but even at their reduced size they were about 750 feet long, 300 feet wide and 100 feet high.

The construction called for an enormous gravel mound to temporarily support a poured in place concrete vault, ten feet thick. One of the most strenuous jobs for the prisoners was the unloading of cement bags from the trains. They were heavy and dusty and had to be carried at a fast pace. If a bag broke, it created a huge mess; cement dust got everywhere, in their eyes, noses and mouths, in their hair, and in their clothing. And as already mentioned, they couldn't get another set of clothes or adequately wash up. Dad, Al and Yechiel managed to avoid the task of carrying cement bags, most of the time.

These huge bunkers had each been contracted out to different firms for construction, and with the use of concentration camp prisoners (i.e. slaves) they saved millions of Reichsmarks. But by the end of the war only one of the three bunkers was close to completion (it is currently the home of a German Air Force repair facility), and barely a trace of the other two remains. Unlike other companies, those particular firms have steadfastly refused to pay any compensation to their former "laborers."

In fact, the heads of those firms even rose to some prominence in post war Germany.

For the first two or three weeks the men received a barely sufficient ration of food, which led them to believe that their purpose was indeed to work. As time went by, however, the quantity decreased. In general, in the evening they received a slice of bread, which they divided in two, half for dinner and half for the following morning, and some watery soup, which if they found a piece of potato or fish in it they considered themselves lucky. In the morning they received coffee, which they mostly did without, and at midday they again received watery soup. Needless to say, they were always on the look out to "organize" food; a potato peel here or there could make the difference between life and death.

Drinking water was available at the work place on occasion, but they needed permission to obtain the water, which was a twenty-minute walk away. Those selected for this errand, Dad included, had to carry the water back in a huge pail for other prisoners as well, and the cleanliness of the water was questionable.

The hygiene, or lack thereof, was indescribable. They had to wear their filthy clothes on their dirty bodies for months on end. They were granted two showers, at least a two-hour walk each way, and there was barely any hot water. During the entire time they were in the Dachau satellite camps #2 and #11, over nine months, their clothing was changed twice.

Although bathing was basically unheard of, they were required to have a shave. Quite a few barbers were among them, including one from their hometown. The barbers had a razor, a brush and a bar of soap. The prisoners stood in line and the barber shaved a hundred men with the same razor blade. Luckily Dad didn't have to worry about shaving yet.

Dachau

There were no mirrors, so they couldn't see how awful they looked, but they had a sense of it by looking at each other.

Dad was concerned about his hands, which were swollen with terrible looking pustules. He asked Yechiel, who had them too, and he diagnosed them as the result of either malnutrition or infection. Dad decided to see the Jewish camp doctor anyway, even though that was risky. What if he had a communicable disease and they had to quarantine him? The doctor looked at Dad's hands and told him they were infected, as many of the prisoners' hands were, and there was nothing he could do about it, since the Germans didn't provide any medications. In a few weeks his hands got better, but then they got worse, and this cycle repeated itself again and again.

Then there were the lice, which were eating them alive. As Dad said, "It is hard for anyone who has not been exposed to hundreds of lice to comprehend what torture it is." They had lice in their hair and lice in their clothes, especially the seams where the multitudes gathered. At night it was unbearable. They would squeeze the lice with their hands until they fell asleep from exhaustion. Honestly Dad couldn't decide which was worse—the hunger or the lack of hygiene.

To pass what little free time they had in the evenings and on Sundays, they talked. Dad, Al and Yechiel talked a lot about their Mother and Maša. They talked about the food they had before the war, especially Dad who had been such a fussy eater. They also talked a lot about miracles. God had performed miracles for the Jewish people throughout history, saving them from destruction numerous times. Why didn't God put an end to this senseless brutality? Why were there no miracles this time? To this day these questions trouble Dad.

Summer 1944 — Spring 1945

Once Dad made an appeal to me, "Mashki, next time you make Pesach, put a few potato peels on the Seder plate as a reminder of the hard times we had, see if anyone asks what they are doing there." In the concentration camp, if ever they found potato peels, they would boil them making a weak potato soup. It was a meal for them; Dad was almost tempted to call it a delicacy. So Dad wanted me to begin this Pesach tradition to pass on to my son Max, which oddly enough he didn't initiate in his own house while I was growing up. But because we don't typically celebrate the holiday together (he and my stepmom Judy spend it at a kosher-for-Pesach resort), he didn't know I had already come up with a tradition of my own.

For the last few years I've incorporated into our Seder (ceremonial meal), the *Survivor's Haggadah*, a book Dad found while wandering around one of the major bookstores. It was created by, for, and dedicated to the "Saved Remnant," the few Jews who survived. It was meant to be a supplement to the traditional Haggadah (the story of the Jews bondage in, and exodus from, Egypt), interweaving the story of the distant past with the story of the Holocaust. This Haggadah was originally printed by the U.S. Army of Occupation and was used by approximately two hundred Survivors at the Seders at the Theatre Cafe in Munich on April 15 and 16, 1946. It was reprinted in 2000, when a man found it among his father's papers after he had passed away. Of course, Dad never mentioned he attended these Seders; he forgot all about them until reminded by this book.

So right before Max asks the "Four Questions," a duty Dad also had in his family as the youngest, I explain the history of this special Haggadah. I also read a few quotes from it, the following being the most poignant, "When it came time for the young to ask the Questions, the survivor celebrants, becoming aware that there were no children present, fell silent, weeping, until one man began the asking and the rest joined in."

Dachau

Yechiel's oldest brother was also in satellite camp #2, and Dad thought Yechiel would go and stay with him, but he didn't. At least the brother should come and stay with them. He broached the subject with Yechiel, but quickly dropped it when Yechiel said his brother was a kvetch (a complainer). After a couple of months Yechiel's brother got sick and was taken away. Yechiel also had a cousin nearby who specialized in engraving currency plates. He didn't look like he was starving; he wore better clothes and slept in better quarters. Yechiel spoke with him once or twice. Dad asked Yechiel why he didn't ask him for food or cigarettes. But the cousin was forbidden to speak with other prisoners and was scared he would be punished if caught. Only once did the cousin give Yechiel a few cigarettes.

One night Dad lay there unable to fall asleep; his heart was racing and he had a pain in his chest. He told Al, "I think I'm going to die." Al looked at him and said, "Don't worry, you're not going to die, you have to suffer a little more first."

If a prisoner got sick and was admitted to the hospital, it was certain death if he stayed more than two or three days. Nothing was done to help him; he wasn't even fed. He just lay there until he died.

Once Dad really did get sick. After work he came into camp and collapsed with a fever. Then, without telling anybody he dragged himself to the hospital. It was no use, he thought, by morning he would be dead. When Al returned from work, Krotenberg informed him that Dad had "admitted" himself. Al went to Dad and started yelling, "You come back! You come back!" Al then exchanged Dad's food ration with a kitchen helper for two aspirins. Dad couldn't even eat the minuscule amount of food they were given anyway. Dad took the aspirins, and Al took him out of the hospital and back to the barracks. Dad perspired throughout the night as if someone were pouring water on him

Summer 1944 — Spring 1945

with a hose. In the morning he went to work. Al had saved Dad's life. Their Mother had foreseen the day, on the train to Stutthof, when one of them would need the other's help.

Dad hoped he would be assigned to be the assistant for a steam shovel operator, so he could be relieved of carrying cement bags all day. He also hoped that by working closer with a German civilian he might have a chance to obtain some extra food. Other prisoners warned him that some of the civilians were just as bad as the SS, but Dad was skeptical.

One day Dad was randomly taken out of line; he had gotten his wish. When Dad saw the Nazi party emblem on the lapel of the steam shovel operator he knew he'd have to be alert. Still, Dad thought, the operator might have children his age; he might feel sympathetic enough to bring him some food. Each morning Dad greeted him as cheerfully as he could, but the operator never replied. Once Dad asked him for his leftovers, and the operator yelled at Dad that he should never speak to him again.

The operator only gave Dad orders, and Dad learned fast not to ask him twice. It was very hard for Dad to understand his "hillbilly" dialect, for he came from western Bavaria. But Dad quickly learned the routine required of him. The operator would call out if he wanted to turn right or left, and Dad had to pull the steel levers at the back of the shovel. Sometimes Dad could not engage the arm, the shovel would go too far, and the operator would have to back off and try again. Then he would become enraged, throwing whatever he had handy at Dad. Sometimes Dad didn't engage the arm on purpose.

One day it was pouring rain. All the other operators stopped working. When the dirt and sand got wet the shovels were very difficult to operate. Out of seventy steam shovels (Dad had counted them), Dad's was the only one that continued working. Then the steel cable broke and the bucket came down. The operator

Dachau

yelled at Dad to replace the broken cable. Dad had to climb the bridge arm, over thirty feet in length, carrying a ninety-pound cable and put it through the guide wheel. The bridge arm was slippery, and Dad, always a bit nervous of heights, thought he would surely slip and fall the fifteen feet to the ground and break his neck. He asked the operator if he could wait until the rain stopped and got a five-pound wrench thrown at him. Had he not moved, it would have split his head open. Needless to say, Dad replaced the cable. After working for the operator for another two weeks the engine broke down, and Dad was assigned to dig holes for electrical poles.

While returning from work one day, Dad noticed guards unloading white bread, which was considered a delicacy so he knew it wasn't for the prisoners. Dad was walking with Al and Yechiel, and he was so famished he decided to steal a loaf. All he had to do was run about forty feet, grab a loaf, and run back in line before anyone noticed. Just as Dad picked up a loaf, he had to put it right back down again, for a guard started chasing after him. A few other prisoners had the same idea, but Dad was the only one who actually got caught. Al politely asked the guard not to report Dad, explaining that Dad was young and stupid. The guard promised, but as soon as they arrived at the gate the guard turned him in anyway.

    They put Dad in the space between the inner electrified fence and the outer barbed wire fence. Dad was afraid they were going to hang him. In another camp an eighteen-year-old boy was hung for having cut a blanket into pieces to protect his feet from the cold. Dad contemplated touching the electrified fence to get it over with quickly. Instead, he looked up to a sky colored by the setting sun and saw God sitting amongst the clouds. Instinctively he recited the Shema, the central prayer in Judaism.

Summer 1944 — Spring 1945

Finally, about two hours later, a German guard came out after his supper, ready to execute Dad's punishment. He looked fairly strong dressed in his undershirt, and he carried a chair and a leather whip. Dad would get twenty-five lashes, and if he yelled or talked he would get more. Dad was thrilled—he wasn't going to die!

As the guard whipped him, Dad counted to himself—23, 24, 25, 26, 27...30. Dad thought perhaps he had forgotten to count, so he told the guard he had already given him twenty-five lashes. The guard then gave Dad another twenty-five lashes—for talking. Dad bit his lip to keep from screaming out in pain. Just a couple hundred feet away his brother was watching and waiting for him. Dad could barely move afterward, and Al supported him as they walked back to the barracks together. The next day Dad was back at work; he had no choice, he didn't want to give the guards an excuse to "punish" him again.

On a Sunday in June 2005, Dad stopped by a bakery for a little nosh. He asked the saleswoman how much for the sweet rolls sitting on the counter. She replied that she could not sell them because they had been sitting there since Thursday; she was giving them away. Dad just had to have those rolls and asked if he could take two. She told him to help himself. As Dad walked back to his car with the rolls, he saw himself standing between the electric and barbed wire fences having almost lost his life for attempting to steal a loaf of bread.

While at the work camp, probably in November for it was lightly snowing, Dad noticed that some prisoners had potatoes. When asked, they told him about the farm behind the trees. Farmers kept their potatoes in root cellars to keep them from freezing

Dachau

through the winter. It amazed Dad that these men were able to find the cellar; it was so well concealed.

Dad asked a guard if he could go relieve himself, and he too went to get potatoes. But how many potatoes could he carry? He had no bags. He tucked his shirt into his pants, filled it up with potatoes, and secured it with a rope around his waist. Thirty minutes later he was back at work; the guard didn't realize it had taken him so long since the prisoners all looked the same.

That night Dad, Al and Yechiel made themselves potato soup. However, because they had already eaten their watery soup and half piece of bread, Yechiel suggested they save it for breakfast, hanging the pot over them as they slept. In the morning the pot was there, but the soup was gone.

For the next potato run, Dad suggested to Al that they go together, that way they could get twice as many. Dad knew the procedure; it should be no problem.

Once they reached the place and Dad was about to crawl down inside, they heard yelling from a couple hundred feet away. A German soldier was shouting for them to stop. Immediately they stood up and started running back, and the German started shooting. Dad glanced over his shoulder and saw a dog chasing after them. The shooting didn't scare him that much, but the dog did. If the dog had caught them, he would have torn them apart. Dad yelled to Al to split up. This confused the dog; he stopped and sniffed the ground not knowing which way to go. Dad said he ran so fast he could have won Olympic gold. When they got close to the work area, they slowed to a walk and blended in with the other prisoners.

That same fall Dad's shoes fell apart. He had to attach the soles to the uppers with string, a technique that did not work for long. There was really no way to fix worn out shoes, and the only way to replace them was to take them off a dead prisoner. Somehow

Summer 1944 — Spring 1945

Dad would have to get better shoes if he was going to survive the winter.

Al came up with a plan, albeit temporary. He volunteered to work the night shift so the brothers could pass Al's shoes between them on their way to and from work. It wasn't as easy as it sounds; they each had to be positioned on the outside of a line so that they physically passed each other. As Dad said, "It had to be done with the utmost precision." So for two weeks they shared Al's pair of shoes.

In the meantime, Al asked the German civilian he worked with, maintaining electrical motors, for any pair of shoes he could spare. Even though he would be compensated, the man was hesitant to help; if caught, he'd be sent to the Russian front for helping a Jew. When the weather got really bad, Al pleaded with the man. Finally he brought Al a pair of used shoes with wooden soles and burlap uppers. Dad was disappointed; he expected a shoe of higher quality. After all, they cost him his precious Bar Mitzvah watch (which he had smuggled into camp). But the shoes fit, and he had something on his feet that bitter cold winter.

In all their time at the Dachau satellite camps they received one Red Cross package—it contained chocolate, hard candy, sugar, and sardines; some packages even had cigarettes. The last month in camp the food ration was cut to a single thin slice of stale or moldy bread. There were those who convinced themselves that it was O.K. to eat certain leaves and grasses they found growing nearby. Many did and died as a result.

By the end of April 1945, the prisoners knew the Americans were in Germany, and that they were nearby. One of them had overheard the guards; another had found a piece of newspaper. The Germans were retreating, supposedly to reorganize for an attack, but even the prisoners knew that was nonsense.

Dachau

The Americans had in fact landed in France, at Normandy Beach, almost eleven months prior. It was only a matter of time before the Nazis were defeated—the prisoners just had to stay alive. And by staying alive they were doing their part for the war effort; they were keeping the German soldiers busy guarding them and not fighting the Allies.

DEATH MARCH

✡ ✡ ✡

SPRING 1945

Early one morning the SS issued an order that no one was to leave for work. Instead the German guards took them out of camp, on what came to be known as the "Death March." They were told they were being taken to a work camp deeper in Bavaria, but in fact they were being marched away from the approaching Americans, with guns pointing at them from all directions. The Nazis did not want the evidence of barely living Jews to fall into Allied hands.

    The prisoners marched the entire day without food or water. Those who fell behind, or those who dropped to the ground and could not get up, were shot. They heard shots constantly. Dad became weaker by the hour. When night approached they were walking on a road through a wooded area, and Dad asked if they could attempt an escape. Yechiel convinced him that the time was not right; there were still too many guards around them.

    Late that night they were brought to rest in an open field near Kaufering. Dad knew that he couldn't last much longer without food; his strength was running out. Seeing that the German guards were sleeping not far from them, Dad told Al and Yechiel that he was going to steal a guard's backpack—he was that desperate. He waited for an hour until all was quiet. Around midnight, as the clouds covered the moon, Dad crawled over on his belly to where the guards slept, about a hundred feet away, and very slowly pulled one of their backpacks toward him.

Spring 1945

He returned the same way, crawling backwards, since there was no room to turn around without waking someone.

They waited a bit so as not to arouse suspicion of the guards, or the other prisoners, before they opened the backpack. It contained a few small loaves of bread and four cans of condensed milk, which they divided between the three of them. They ate the biggest portion right away in case they were searched in the morning. With a homemade knife they cut the remaining bread into slices, which they put in their pockets, and they punched holes in the cans. The milk was cold and sweet. Al was ready to toss the unused can of milk, but Dad thought—why should it go to waste? He was still thirsty, so he drank the extra can. Al then threw the backpack with the empty cans into the woods nearby.

At daybreak they heard a guard shouting that the "Damn Jews" had stolen his backpack and the guilty ones would be punished. But there was no search; they just started marching again. Dad was the only one of over a thousand prisoners who had taken such a risk.

After a few hours Dad started feeling a pain in his stomach that got worse by the minute. His stomach, unaccustomed to the condensed milk, felt like it would explode. Every step he took was torture; he could barely walk. All he wanted to do was to lie down and sleep off the pain. Dad told Yechiel that he should walk with Al; Dad would fall behind and try to escape. He didn't want to be a burden. At this point Yechiel and Al grabbed Dad under the arms and helped him walk. Dad continued talking about escaping into the woods when it got dark, but Yechiel said they were just too close to being liberated to take any chances now.

When they came close to Wolfratshausen, the walking became a bit easier. The road was like a downward spiral, the weather was great, and the scenery was the most beautiful Dad had ever seen. Word spread that they would be getting food and water soon, and they did receive a little water, but no food. They rested near

Death March

Wolfratshausen for about an hour before they started marching again. They marched around the town, not through it, but still German civilians came out and watched them. A few townspeople threw pieces of bread to them, but the German guards yelled at them to stay in line. The guards were afraid of the prisoners having any contact with the civilians. If they stopped marching, the guards might lose control and have a riot on their hands.

They marched again late into the evening, past Wolfratshausen and Icking, and stopped somewhere near Fohrenwald, where there were some empty prisoner barracks. It was very crowded and some prisoners had to sleep outside on the grass.

Dad got up early the next morning. He didn't feel quite so sick, but he knew he couldn't walk another day, not without collapsing and getting shot. He went to the latrine to take a discreet look around. Through the fog he saw a few homes scattered across the road. He also kept his eye on the guards, whose numbers had diminished a bit from the previous day, and soon they gathered to make their plans. From inside the latrine, with its angled slats, Dad could see and hear the guards perfectly, but they couldn't see him. Dad heard them say that they would start marching again as soon as the fog lifted, and Dad realized this was it, his only chance to escape. When their meeting broke up and the guards dispersed, his chance would be lost.

He didn't even have time to tell Al and Yechiel. Dad crossed the road and thought that if the guards yelled for him to stop, he wouldn't turn around; he'd just keep on going. If they shot him in the back, it was fine with him. But the guards didn't even notice him. Dad went to the first house he saw, a couple hundred feet from the road, and rang the rear doorbell.

Dad had clearly taken a chance. A dog might have come after him or started barking, alerting the neighbors. Dad had no idea who would open that door, and there he was—dressed in his striped uniform.

A nicely dressed, good-looking woman of about thirty-five answered the door. Dad told her who he was and asked if he could stay in her basement overnight. He didn't need food, he knew food was scarce for the Germans too; he only needed to sleep. She invited him into the kitchen and offered him some food anyway. Dad was embarrassed by how dirty he was and he told her so, but she insisted he come in anyway. She served him bread, butter, cheese and salami. Later she brought him coffee. Dad asked her not to mention his presence to the neighbors, and she told him not to worry. Then she left Dad in the kitchen. Dad was more interested in the food than in where she had gone.

After a few minutes she returned with apples and left again. Dad looked through the open door into a lovely living room, filled with beautiful furniture and Persian rugs, a different world, with no sign of misery. An hour later the doorbell rang. Dad asked if he should go to the basement. The woman told him not to be frightened; it was just a neighbor. Dad then realized that she had left to call a neighbor, and anyone in her position would have done the same. Dad didn't like the neighbor being there; he didn't want to become the subject of gossip. If the whole village knew about him, he would be in even greater danger.

The woman sat down at the table with Dad and asked about the concentration camp and the conditions there. Dad replied that it would be difficult for her to understand, or even believe, the conditions and the cruelty without seeing it firsthand. Dad was hesitant to say more; he didn't want to scare or offend her by being too graphic. He also didn't want her to throw him out of her house, thinking he was insane. The woman suggested that Dad change clothes and brought him a complete outfit—shirt and tie, suit, trench coat and hat, shoes and socks, even underwear. She also brought a pail of water and wanted to wash his feet, but Dad refused to let her. She left Dad alone in the kitchen to wash up. Dad asked where he should dispose of his lice infested clothing, and she indicated the coal furnace in the basement. After changing his clothes and stilling his hunger, Dad felt like a human being again and looked more like a reporter than a prisoner. He even felt safe in the house knowing the Americans were close by, and liberation was at hand. He believed that this German woman welcomed him into her home to show the Americans that she and her family had helped a Jew. Dad and the woman talked for a good part of the day, and so he didn't get any sleep after all.

After six o'clock her husband came home; he was a scientist and worked in a nearby laboratory. When he took off his coat Dad saw the Nazi party emblem on his lapel and knew he had chosen the wrong house. The woman explained who Dad was and the husband began shouting, "Damn Jew, if you do not disappear from this house immediately, I will call the police!" He even blamed Dad for Germany losing the war. His wife did not intervene when he shouted at Dad. She had been nice and polite all day, and Dad thanked her for her kindness. He left the house scared, pleading for him not to call the police.

When Dad looked down the road he saw German soldiers, motorcycles, trucks and half-tracks retreating. He was unable to cross the road and he could not go back to the house; he was caught in no man's land. He walked slowly as he pondered his next move. Then he heard footsteps and turned around to see the woman of the house hurrying after him. Dad's first impression was that maybe her husband had changed his mind. She told Dad that she had just heard on the radio that the Americans were in Munich, and there was a good possibility that they would be here by morning. She suggested Dad cross the road; there was an old shack in the woods where Dad could stay overnight. The problem was how to cross without being noticed. Dad asked the woman for a newspaper. He thought he'd be less conspicuous if he were reading the paper, rather than watching the Germans

Spring 1945

retreat. Dad made a hole in the newspaper to keep watch for a break in the traffic, while he leaned against a big tree. He was far from the road and doubted he was even seen as the vehicles sped by at thirty to forty miles per hour. After about half an hour the traffic let up, and Dad slowly crossed the road. He continued to read his newspaper until he disappeared into the woods.

He did not go to the shack; the husband might still change his mind and call the police. Dad went deeper into the woods until he found a patch of grass surrounded by some bushes; there he lay down. For a while Dad listened to the noise of the trucks and watched flashes of gunfire bombarding the night sky in the vicinity of Munich. When it quieted down he fell asleep. He awoke feeling guilty that he had escaped; he was worried about Al and Yechiel. What was he going to tell his Mother? She had asked them to stay together. He decided to wait until sunrise and then walk back to the barracks where he had left them the night before.

When Dad neared the barracks he saw several prisoners milling about. He approached very slowly; the closer he got to camp the more concerned he became for his safety. After all, he wasn't wearing the striped uniform anymore. The prisoners might mistake him for a German civilian in his newly acquired clothes, and before he could open his mouth they would kill him. He removed his hat so they could see his short hair. On his way he encountered Russian prisoners and asked them where the other prisoners were staying. They answered that they were in the barracks, and that most of the guards had changed into civilian clothes and left. That only increased Dad's anxiety, now the prisoners might mistake him for a German guard. Dad saw a few guards remaining, without their rifles, but they weren't bothering anybody, and nobody was bothering them.

Dad entered the barracks and found his brother and brother-in-law lying on the floor with other prisoners. They hugged and kissed, and Dad told them about his great adventure. They told

Death March

him he looked good, at least compared to everyone else. A Jewish kapo approached and offered Dad two loaves of bread for the suit. Dad conferred with Al and Yechiel, and they said Dad should keep his clothes—he earned them. They'd get bread soon enough. (I remember Unc telling me, shaking his head with a smile on his face, how bizarre it was to see Dad saunter into the barracks in a suit.)

Late that morning they heard the grinding sound of an approaching tank, and for a few moments Dad thought it was German. As it came out of the woods, gun barrel first, they didn't see a swastika, but a star on its front. Still, Dad hesitated to come close. The soldiers, sitting on top of the tank, threw Hershey's chocolate bars down to them. Dad picked one up and with tears running down his face cried, "Why did it take you so long?" Dad is not sure if he said those words aloud or just in his head. Dad, Al, Yechiel, and the others who survived with them, were liberated by the Americans on May 1, 1945. The war in Europe officially ended one week later.

ICKING

✣ ✣ ✣

SPRING — SUMMER 1945

For the first couple of days, the prisoners, now "Survivors," were basically on their own, but the Americans organized fairly quickly. They set up a Displaced Persons (DP) camp in Fohrenwald, in housing originally built for construction workers of IG Farben. Most of the Survivors were transported there in trucks, but those who could walk did so, including Dad, Al and Yechiel, and they didn't have to wait.

Hundreds of thousands of Jewish Survivors stayed in DP camps from 1945 through 1952, although Fohrenwald was the last to close in 1957. Governments sent transportation to bring their citizens home—but no one came for the Jews. Besides, few Jews wanted to return to the home countries that had betrayed them. And few other countries were willing to increase their immigration quotas at the end of the war. It wasn't until 1948 that the United States increased its quotas, and by then most of the Jews had already gone to the newly established State of Israel.

Before entering the DP camp, the Survivors were sprayed with delousing solution. Finally they received the help they so desperately needed—food (which got better by the day), clothing (surplus army fatigues and civilian clothes), medicine, blankets and cots.

The camp was very crowded. Brick walls enclosed the entire complex, and soon Dad and Al went to see what was beyond those walls. Outside they found a structure almost completely

Spring — Summer 1945

underground. As they wandered from room to room, separated by steel doors, they saw microscopes, tubes and gadgets. They realized they were in some sort of chemical laboratory or factory, and they were spooked. They were also afraid those steel doors would automatically close, and they would be entombed in there forever. Even so, Dad and Al went back later for a second look, but they found the place had been almost entirely emptied out.

After one week, Dad and his friend Isaac (from the Shavl ghetto) decided it was time to obtain some transportation. Before sunrise they left the DP camp and headed for a nearby village. On the way they saw a small fire in the woods. They went to investigate and found some black American soldiers warming themselves around a flaming metal barrel, with guns in hand, and blankets around their shoulders. Dad and Isaac stayed with them for a while. The soldiers were shivering, which surprised the two of them because they weren't dressed nearly as warmly, but perhaps the soldiers had been out there all night. Dad and Isaac were astonished at how dark the soldiers' skin was, and they were amazed that the soldiers hadn't ask them any questions—after all, they could have been Nazis.

When the sky lightened Dad and Isaac continued on, and like others before them, they went house to house in search of what they needed. Dad felt no guilt in asking for a bicycle; after all, the Nazis had stolen his. Eventually they were successful. They acquired two bicycles, not in the best condition, but at least they had the means to get to Munich, if they didn't get a flat along the way.

They never made it to the big city. It took only an hour for them to become thirsty, hungry, and tired. They rode mostly uphill on the very same spiral road they had "marched" down only a short time ago. On a hilltop they found American Military Police (MPs), who looked them over, but didn't bother them.

Icking

They pedaled on, and in a few miles they came to an American command post, comprised of tents and some German homes, in and around the small town of Icking.

Icking was a beautiful place, overlooking the Isar River, with a distant view of the Alps, about a half hour drive from Munich. It was here that the rich had built their villas, including some high-ranking German officers.

Dad suggested to Isaac that they stop at the command post and ask for some work. Ideally they were hoping to find a Jewish American soldier so they could converse in Yiddish, the universal Jewish language. Their English wasn't the best, but they could make themselves understood. Actually, Dad had asked his Father to teach him some English when they were still in the ghetto; he thought that after the war he might like to go to America or England.

They approached a soldier that Dad thought might be Jewish, which he was, but he couldn't speak or understand Yiddish. The soldier told them that when he was young he used to go to his grandmother's for dinner on Friday night and eat gefilte fish; that was the extent of his Jewishness. He asked about their parents. Although they didn't know for certain, Dad and Isaac presumed that the Nazis had killed them. Then the soldier called over to his buddy and said, "Hey Fritz, look what your landsmen did to these people." Dad and Isaac were embarrassed. Fritz wore an American soldier's uniform, so as far as they were concerned he was an American.

Dad realized he wasn't going to get anywhere with that particular soldier, so he approached another. He too was Jewish—and he knew Yiddish. He was a Sergeant from Brooklyn and he was very friendly. Dad asked him if there was any work for them in the kitchen. The Sergeant went to ask the Master Sergeant in charge of the kitchen detail, and a few minutes later he returned with jobs for them. They could begin right away. These weren't paying positions, but there were benefits.

Spring — Summer 1945

Dad and Isaac were given permission to eat whatever remained—cooked cereal, powdered eggs, grits, bacon, pancakes and more. Dad tried the golden brown pancakes, which he stacked like a seven layer cake with jam and syrup. They were delicious; he ate so many he thought his stomach would burst. At that rate he would quickly gain the weight he should have been carrying on his growing 5'-10" frame.

Their job was to clean the pots and pans; the three hundred soldiers would take care of their own mess kits. A cook showed them how to wash with hot water, rinse with hot water, and then rinse with cold water. But first—Dad and Isaac had to throw whatever food remained into the garbage (a large pit in the ground that was burned every other day). How long had they starved—and now they were throwing food away!

When Dad and Isaac were done cleaning it was time for the cooks to start preparing lunch—hot dogs and some other meat, mashed potatoes, canned vegetables, two kinds of soup, coffee with condensed milk, powdered milk, and hot cocoa. Again, when it was time to clean up, there was uneaten food. Dad put some of this excess food to good use—he brought it to the DP camp for Al, Yechiel, and some friends. Unfortunately, he could only carry so much on his bicycle. For two weeks Isaac also brought food back to camp, until his uncle from South Africa came for him. Dad worked in the kitchen for a few months, until the Americans left Icking in early autumn.

It didn't take long before Dad became a favorite among the American soldiers, and he developed a thriving business in Icking and the surrounding villages. A soldier would ask Dad if he knew someone who could repair a watch, and Dad would hop on his bicycle to search for a watchmaker in Wolfratshausen. Sometimes soldiers dropped in on Thursdays to see if Dad could get a hold of some schnapps for the weekend. The soldiers paid Dad with cigarettes, coffee or chocolate. Dad extracted a fee for his services,

Icking

and everyone was happy. Occasionally he was even paid in cash, not that Dad had any idea how much a dollar was worth, but he took whatever they gave him. Dad also arranged for German women to wash and iron the soldiers' uniforms. He did not take a fee for this small service, since he didn't want to be bothered with pick-up and delivery.

Once an American Lieutenant asked Dad if he knew someone who could make him a pair of military boots, but of softer leather. By this time Dad knew of a shoemaker in Wolfratshausen, but he wasn't about to reveal his source, so he told the Lieutenant he would ask around. Dad went to the shoemaker and explained that he needed a pair of boots for an American "General," who was understandably too busy to come himself. The shoemaker demonstrated how to measure the foot and ankle, as he placed Dad's bare foot on a piece of paper and traced its contour with a pencil. He told Dad how much leather he would need, and explained that if the General wanted a very high quality boot he would need a greater amount of material, and that there would be considerable waste for he would need to cut from the center.

A couple of days later, Dad returned to the shoemaker with the material and the measurements. Dad asked if there would be enough leftover for a pair of shoes. The shoemaker replied that there would even be enough for another pair of boots. In no time at all the Lieutenant slipped on his brand new boots. Admiring them, he tipped Dad a carton of cigarettes. The shoemaker was paid in cigarettes and coffee, real coffee, not the ersatz coffee the Germans had been drinking for years made of vegetables. And Dad, in addition to his fee and his tip, had a handsome new pair of brown leather boots, Russian style (up to the knee), to strut around Germany in.

While trying to drum up some business, Dad came upon a small house, adjacent to a long, beautiful, tree lined driveway. Dad

Spring — Summer 1945

knocked on the door and gave the old man who answered his sales pitch, and they struck a deal—coffee for schnapps. The old man volunteered that he was only the gardener for the Sanatorium, which lay at the end of the three hundred foot drive. It was owned by a medical doctor, a former Major in the SS. Dad asked if he ever saw the doctor in his uniform, and the old man replied that he had, many times. The old man had no great love for the doctor, who didn't treat him very nicely. Dad jotted down the doctor's name, got on his bicycle and rode down the driveway.

Dad entered the Sanatorium's large foyer; the place was magnificent, so clean even the floors shined. Dad saw many young children, two to six-years-old, and nurses in starched white uniforms. They were just finishing lunch, eating oranges and bananas in May! The head nurse, an older woman, approached Dad. He inquired after the doctor in charge and was told he was out-of-town for the day. Dad left disappointed.

The following day Dad saw the "boots" Lieutenant and told him about this SS officer. After lunch, the Lieutenant, Dad, and a driver hopped in a jeep, and Dad directed them to the Sanatorium. Dad spoke with the nurse and she led them to the doctor's office. The doctor presented his release papers from the Wehrmacht, and although the Lieutenant didn't read German, he was satisfied that everything was in order. Dad tried to nose his way in on the conversation, but the Lieutenant would have none of it. He simply apologized for the inconvenience and they left.

Dad was livid! How can an SS officer just walk around free! Since Dad didn't get any satisfaction from the "boots" Lieutenant, he went to the Burgermeister, the Mayor of Icking, the very next day.

Dad asked the Burgermeister if he was aware that the doctor of the nearby Sanatorium had been an officer in the SS. The Burgermeister recalled seeing the Major in his SS uniform. Dad asked if he could get that in writing. Immediately the Burgermeister called in his secretary and gave her a statement to type, which he then signed and sealed. Once Dad had that

Icking

document in hand he went straight to the military police at Wolfratshausen.

Within ten minutes they assembled a Sergeant and two MPs, all wearing helmets and toting guns. Dad drove with them to the Sanatorium and told the nurse they needed to see the doctor at once. He wasn't in the office, but at home, in another big beautiful villa, located directly behind the Sanatorium.

The maid opened the door and went to inform the doctor he had visitors. But Dad was right on her heels; he couldn't wait, let alone run the risk of the doctor slipping out the back. He barged right into the library and proceeded to interrogate the doctor as he thrust the Burgermeister's document toward him. The doctor confirmed it was true; he had been a member of the Nazi party and an SS officer. The MPs told the doctor it was time for him to come with them, but they allowed him to telephone his wife first. Dad overheard their conversation—the doctor thought it was just "routine." "Enough talking," Dad said as he grabbed the receiver and hung it up. The doctor changed out of his white coat and they walked out to the jeep.

Dad sat cramped in the back seat, with an MP, and the doctor between them. As they pulled away Dad started yelling at the doctor, "How did it feel to kill women and children!" Dad shook him—he was ready to strangle him, but the MP yelled at Dad, "You can't do that, the court will decide what to do with him!" The doctor defended himself saying he was not at the front; he didn't kill anyone. He just took care of the children.

When they arrived at MP headquarters, Dad saw a familiar face, a civilian and fellow prisoner of Dachau. He was a nice-looking, gentile Czech, who spoke both English and German fluently. Dad showed him the statement from the Burgermeister of Icking, and the man said he would take it from there.

Dad later learned the doctor served a five-year sentence, and of course, the children he was taking such good care of were the offspring of other SS officers.

Spring — Summer 1945

One day an idea hit Dad. The soldiers were always drinking coffee, at least three times a day, and the coffee grounds that sat at the bottom of the pot were just thrown away. Dad took the used grounds and spread them out to dry on any kind of paper he could find. It was summer so they dried fairly quickly. He purchased some paper bags from the corner store and filled them with the dried grounds. He then rode his bicycle to the first house he saw and told the residents that he had not one, but two grades of coffee to sell. (The second grade of coffee was his own "special blend," while the first grade was what the soldiers had given him in exchange for the schnapps.) He opened a bag of the second grade coffee and told his potential customers to sample it. "Isn't it wunderbar!" they exclaimed. They loved it, and for a third of the price of the first grade coffee. Dad was in the coffee business, decades before Starbucks; he was so busy he almost had to hire someone to help with production.

One evening the Master Sergeant in charge of the kitchen detail, a short, husky man with a moustache, asked Dad if he would like to help him and his assistant catch a sheep. The Sergeant was tired of eating canned food; he had a taste for fresh meat. At midnight they hopped into a military jeep and drove to where a herd of about 150 sheep were corralled. It was like a three-ring circus with the three of them chasing the sheep, and the sheep running away from them. They almost gave up, but eventually they managed to catch one and put it in a big burlap sack.

They drove back to the kitchen and the Sergeant proceeded to slaughter the animal. As Dad watched the blood come pouring out, he began staggering; he was about to faint. A couple of soldiers held him up, while one of them took out a cigarette, lit it, and gave it to him—it would make him feel better. That was Dad's first cigarette, and it nearly choked him. (Still, it proved to be the beginning of a bad habit that lasted many years, well

Icking

into my childhood.) Dad didn't look when the Sergeant carved up the flesh, and after the sheep was prepared, Dad ate the same old hotdogs—he couldn't bring himself to eat the poor sheep.

Later on this same Sergeant asked Dad if he wanted to go for a ride with him to pick up supplies. Dad jumped at the opportunity to see the devastation that was once Munich. The majority of the buildings had been destroyed, and it gave Dad pleasure to see that the Americans had done such a good job.

On the return trip, the Sergeant asked Dad if he knew how to drive. Dad was too embarrassed to say he did not. Besides, Dad always said "yes" at this point in his life; "no" wasn't part of his vocabulary, "no" didn't open any doors.

The Sergeant stopped the truck and they switched seats. Dad had ridden with the American soldiers many times, so he figured—how hard could driving be? Dad drove for about a minute, swaying right and left, before the Sergeant realized that Dad was going to get them killed. The Sergeant yelled, with expletives, for Dad to stop the truck, and he jerked it to a halt with the clutch still in. Dad's excuse—he wasn't accustomed to American trucks. They switched seats again, and needless to say, there wasn't much conversation for the remainder of the trip.

One day in Wolfratshausen, just as Dad was going into a store, he recognized the woman coming out. She was the nice lady who had opened her home to him after he had escaped from the Death March. She told Dad that when the Russian prisoners were liberated they came to her house, plundered everything, and killed her husband. It occurred to Dad that her story might simply be a fabrication to protect her husband—afraid that Dad would come after him. Dad could not reconcile her kindness with her husband's hatred. Perhaps she wouldn't have been so kind if the Americans hadn't been so close. Yet

Spring — Summer 1945

her husband knew the war was lost, and still he clung to his hatred of the Jews. In a gesture of thanks, Dad handed her the oranges he was going to bring to the DP camp. A couple of weeks passed and Dad rode his bicycle out to the house, only to find it empty. It occurred to him later that he did not even know the woman's name.

Dad stayed in the DP camp for just a few weeks. He had no interest in staying there any longer. He had enough of camps. Since he spent a lot of time riding his bicycle from Fohrenwald to Icking and back, he thought it would be much more convenient to live in Icking.

For a week he stayed with some American soldiers, in one of their confiscated houses, before he secured other living arrangements. For that he sought the help of the Burgermeister, with whom he was acquainted from the business with the Sanatorium SS doctor. Dad explained that he was working for the Americans and needed to live closer to them. He also asked if the Burgermeister could find accommodations for his brother, brother-in-law and some friends.

The Burgermeister offered Dad a house where they could all live together, but Dad felt a house filled only with Jews was just asking for trouble. Dad simply wanted to rent rooms and live among the Germans. The Burgermeister made some calls, and in no time Dad came to live on the second floor of the home of a former German officer in the Wehrmacht, by the name of Kaltenegger. Dad lived there, on and off, from 1945 through 1948. The rent was cheap, and it was a nice place to go to on the weekends.

About a month after liberation, when Yechiel had regained enough strength, he and another man decided to return to Lithuania to find their wives. Dad and Al also wanted to go, but Yechiel felt they would be a hindrance. A lot of people were traveling from

Icking

country to country at that time, and it was hard to get transportation. This time it was Dad who had the currency for the journey, and he gave Yechiel cigarettes, chocolate and a few watches. The only identification they had were their Dachau certificates, stating their name, age and birthplace, signed by the American officer who had liberated them.

Yechiel and his traveling companion hitched rides from American soldiers and German farmers until they reached a Jewish DP camp near Hanover. It took them ten days, where nowadays it would take five-and-a-half hours on the Autobahn. There they met a few Jewish women from Shavl. The women informed them that traveling to Soviet occupied Lithuania was risky; it would be easy for them to get in, but very difficult to get out. And sad to say, they no longer had a reason to go.

The women knew with certainty that their wives and mother-in-law had perished at Stutthof concentration camp. Maša could have survived by continuing on in the work camp near Stutthof, but when her Mother's feet froze and she could no longer work, she was shipped back to Stutthof. Maša, not wanting her Mother to be alone, accompanied her, and both were killed there. The Yahrtzeit of Chaya Rachel Pruchno and Maša Saks, the anniversary of their deaths, has always been observed on December 7, 1944.

It took Yechiel two weeks to return to Fohrenwald, and he arrived dirty and exhausted. (The other man continued on to Poland, to see what, if anything, he could salvage of his pre-war wealth.) When Yechiel conveyed the heartbreaking news, Dad cried hysterically. He was angry and depressed, and felt lost knowing both his parents were now gone. He was anxious about the future, but remembering his Father's dying words about honesty gave him some comfort.

Soon a rumor circulated that the American soldiers were going to seal off the DP camp, and the inhabitants would only be allowed out with a special permit. Dad urged Al and Yechiel to join him in Icking. If they didn't like it, they could always return to the camp. As Survivors they were entitled to double food rations, which still weren't enough, but with Dad's supplement from the kitchen, they wouldn't starve. So they agreed. Dad also invited Feivel Krotenberg and his wife. Dad really liked Feivel; he was the very nice man who had cut their bread rations at Dachau.

Dad enlisted the aid of an American soldier with access to a jeep, and late one afternoon they drove up to the DP camp gate. The soldier was from the same unit as the guards, so they were allowed to pass through, no questions asked. Dad felt like a big shot being driven through camp to pick up Al and Yechiel (and a few days later, the Krotenbergs). They each grabbed a bag with their few articles of clothing, hopped into the jeep, and off they went.

Icking

```
Camp Office of Dachau        Date  21.6.1945

                    Certificate

                                  Pruchno
It is hereby certified that Mr. ...............
         Samuel          born      1.6.1927
....................,           ..............
    Schaulen
in ..................., was detained in Dachau
Concentration Camp from  22.VII.1944. to the day
of deliverance by the United States Army and was
registered in the Camp Books under the number ..
    84782         He came from   KL.Stutthof
..............                   ..............

                    Camp Office

ROBERT E. SEAL                / Pomagala Jan /
    Capt. A.
C. B., U.S. Team 104      Camp Secretary of Dachau
```

Temporary Identification Certificate

Spring — Summer 1945

Sam Pruchno—Dad
in striped uniform borrowed for picture after the war.

Identification Card

117

MUNICH

✯ ✯ ✯

FALL 1945 — FALL 1951

Yechiel stayed in Icking with Dad and Al for about a month. Then one day he went to Munich; the Jewish Committee was forming. One of the services they were organizing was a weekly Jewish newspaper. Yechiel knew some people and got a job as a reporter. He wrote his articles primarily in Yiddish, and once in a while in English, which he knew from his time in South Africa. His salary wasn't much, but he got benefits—food rations, cigarettes, and packages from an American organization. Yechiel rented a room on the Kolner Platz in the Schwabing area from a Mrs. Krauter; she was an older woman and lived with her daughter, who worked in hospital administration.

Al soon followed Yechiel to Munich and lived with him while he prepared for his exams to enter the University of Munich's engineering school. If he did well enough he would be granted admission as part of reparations. Al worked very hard, making up for his lost years. He stayed up late at night studying, which annoyed Yechiel who couldn't sleep with the light on. He then tried to study in the kitchen, which angered Mrs. Krauter because electricity cost so much. Al got fed up with having to tip-toe around. Once he was enrolled in the university and received a stipend, he moved out. He rented a little room on Baumgart-nerstrasse, a thirty-minute ride from Yechiel's on the #8 street-car. (Unc and I had a standing joke about who attended the real U of M, the University of Munich or the University of Michigan.)

Munich

When the Americans left Icking in September 1945, the Sergeant wanted to ensure that Dad had a roof over his head. (He didn't know Dad was living in Icking.) So he informed the German owner of the house they were vacating that Dad was entitled to stay as long as he liked. Dad thought he'd give it a try. He might like this place better; there was a lot more room. But that first night in the big empty house, Dad was scared to death. The shutter outside the open window creaked back and forth all night long, conjuring up ghosts. Dad stayed just one more night.

With the Americans gone, Dad went to Munich quite frequently to see Al and Yechiel. He enjoyed going out to lunch with them, compiling their ration coupons to put together a decent meal. They also went to the movies, which were always packed.

In the fall of 1946, Dad enrolled in a trade school in Munich, as with Al it was part of reparations. Dad didn't have the option of attending university; he was too young when the war brought a halt to his education. He went to trade school on a part time basis for three years, from the end of 1946 through 1949. Dad was mechanically inclined, and if there was one thing he had learned in the ghettos and the camps—it was good to have a trade. There were approximately one thousand students in the school, however, only twenty or so were Jews, and they were in a separate class. Most of the instructors for the Jewish students were Jewish, but a few were German. Dad got along fine with the German instructors; he offered them American cigarettes.

For a class project Dad "turned," on a lathe, a small pair of steel Shabbat candlesticks. Many years later he located them in a box in the bowels of his basement and had them engraved with the words, "To my daughter Marcia and my grandson Max and all the generations I didn't dare to dream would follow in 1945." I use them every Shabbat, and even though my husband would like a more substantial pair, like the one my Dad had growing up, I'm not interested.

Fall 1945 — Fall 1951

It wasn't long before Dad became acquainted with a German named Herbert Geberbauer, whom he met at the guesthouse in Icking. He lived near Pforzheim, in the French zone. After the war Germany was divided into four zones, American, English, French and Russian. Public transportation was very poor, and Herbert saw an opportunity to make some good money. All he needed was a bus, and he knew exactly where to buy it, but like everyone else he was just short on funds. Herbert asked Dad if he knew someone who might want to go into business with him. Dad suggested that he had some free time—why not show him the bus.

They drove in Herbert's car, an Adler, from Munich to Passau on the Austrian border. There, some Hungarian officers and soldiers, who had collaborated with the Nazis, had stayed on after the war, not wanting to return home to Soviet occupied Hungary. They still had in their possession the German buses and trucks they had used during the war, and they were trying to sell them, without any type of ownership papers. Herbert showed Dad the bus—a beautiful Mercedes. Herbert took it for a test drive and immediately fell in love. He told Dad that if Dad bought him the bus, he would give Dad his car as commission. Dad told him to keep his car—he would buy his own car.

A Hungarian Major, who was in the Luftwaffe (German Air Force), wanted $1200 for the bus, in American dollars only. Dad quietly asked Herbert how much money he had; Herbert only had $260 worth of German marks. Dad told the Major that he came from the English zone; therefore he had only English pounds and not American dollars, which the Major found totally understandable. They did the math, converting dollars to pounds, and shook hands on the deal. Dad and Herbert would return in a few days with the money to make the exchange.

Back in Icking, Dad used Herbert's marks and some of his own money to buy English "pounds"—counterfeit money on the black

Munich

market. During the war the Germans had printed pounds to drop on England in an attempt to destroy its economy, and even an expert had trouble seeing the difference.

The Major also had a camera he wanted to sell. He had used it to take pictures from his airplane, after he had dropped his bombs. Dad described it to Yechiel, who told him it was a bargain at $120, so Dad decided to purchase the camera as well.

Later in the week they were on their way back to Passau with the money and a driver. The driver's instructions were simple—put on the license plates, check the air pressure in the tires, and get the bus the hell out of there. Dad and Herbert would leave later, after they had wined and dined the Hungarian Major, and the driver had put a good distance between them. Everything went smoothly. As Dad and Herbert drove back to Munich, Dad wondered how long it would take the Major to realize he had been duped. Whether he did or not, Dad enjoyed the fact that he had outwitted the "enemy." Herbert was so impressed with Dad's ingenuity that he offered Dad a partnership in his trucking company.

Dad discussed the business proposition with Yechiel. He liked the idea, so Dad introduced the two men, and they all agreed on the following arrangement. Dad and Yechiel would put up forty percent of the money; Herbert would put up thirty percent and draw a salary for taking care of the operational portion of the business. (During the war he had been in charge of transportation for his unit in the Wehrmacht.) They found another German who would put up the remaining thirty percent, and he would draw a salary for taking care of the office, including the bookkeeping. Dad and Yechiel didn't have anything to do with the day-to-day operations of the business; although Dad did plenty of work, he didn't want to commit himself. Being a student, he didn't have much time, and he didn't want to travel to the French zone regularly, where he'd need a special permit, although he did sneak in from time to time.

They went to a lawyer and drew up a contract. Dad did all the legwork, but they put the business in Yechiel's name. Dad thought it looked more impressive to the authorities with an older man's signature. Besides, he trusted Yechiel and wanted to give him the koved (honor). Dad still had the papers when he came to the States, but after carrying them from one place to another he eventually threw them away.

Herbert wanted French-made cars next, for the French officers who didn't want German cars because they couldn't get German spare parts. The first Citroen they acquired was in pretty bad shape. But after they paid one hundred dollars to overhaul the engine, furnish new upholstery, and provide a fresh coat of paint, it was like new. And since the officers didn't have cash, they paid in French cognac. Herbert got between forty and forty-five bottles of cognac per car, depending on its condition. Dad then sold the cognac to a bar in Munich where the owner gave him four to five dollars per bottle. Dad couldn't understand why the American soldiers were so crazy for cognac.

After the Citroens, Herbert wanted a large truck to establish a shipping route between Frankfurt and Hamburg, another potential source of steady income. According to Herbert the best truck for this purpose was a Krupp. It was a husky, German-made truck that ran on diesel and was capable of pulling two trailers. Dad found such a truck, and although it was in terrible condition, there were a lot of spare parts scattered around it that would likely prove useful. It took many months to rebuild, but the truck was like new when it was done. At that time after the war, there was no such thing as buying a new car or truck.

Herbert was a married man, but that didn't stop him from fooling around with the daughter of the owner of the Icking guesthouse. He told her he would divorce his wife and marry

Munich

her, but of course that never happened. Dad thought he just wanted free room and board.

Soon Herbert started drinking a lot. When he came to Munich, he stayed with a friend, and the two of them drank night and day. The friend owned a factory that reconditioned tires (put new coatings on old tires), since new tires weren't available either.

Dad wasn't there when Herbert picked a fight with Yechiel. After Herbert uttered those hateful words—"Damn Jew!"—Yechiel gave him an ultimatum. Either he could buy them out or they would buy him out. Herbert chose to buy them out.

Dad and Yechiel were glad to be done with Herbert; they knew they wouldn't stay in Germany permanently. And Herbert was pleased his company was now entirely German owned and operated. Later, in 1949, Dad heard that Herbert had gone bankrupt, apparently he was not getting along with his German partner either, and he was still drinking heavily.

One summer day in 1947, Dad was in school, standing at the open window with his instructor, when a two-seater Mercedes convertible pulled up. Dad exclaimed that one day he was going to own a car like that. His instructor mentioned that the car belonged to his brother-in-law who was moving to South America; he needed to sell it and was asking three hundred dollars.

Dad called his friend Joe Dembo to see if he would split the cost with him. Joe agreed, even though he didn't know how to drive. Dad had finally learned; Herbert had taught him. Herbert had also gotten Dad license plates, which were not available for private cars. Only business owners could obtain them, and although Yechiel was a co-owner, he did not reside in the French zone where the business was located, and he did not know the right people. Dad and Joe owned that car for only six weeks before they had to sell it; they just couldn't afford to keep it.

Fall 1945 — Fall 1951

They sold it to a Jewish man who was himself just learning how to drive. Part of the deal was that Dad would drive with him for the first month, which was fine with Dad, at least he got to ride in the car a little while longer. The man always wanted to go somewhere. Once they even went to Nuremberg, about a hundred miles away, just to see a soccer match.

That was Dad's first car, one of five that he owned in Germany. It was easier to place Dad's stories in chronological order knowing which car he drove at the time.

Dad had met Joe Dembo when they both worked for the Americans, since they provided similar services. Joe worked in Bad Tolz and he came to Icking, fifteen miles away, once or twice a week with the soldiers. Dad and Joe even did some business together. One of their customers was the young, good-looking wife of the naval architect who built the passenger ship, the *Bremen*. Joe was acquainted with their son, and they owned the nicest villa in the area. It was a log structure with a balcony encircling it, big picture windows facing the incredible view, and the largest kitchen Dad ever saw, six times the size of a typical 1970s suburban kitchen.

The wife wanted to sell some jewelry to obtain food on the black market. She gave Dad and Joe a diamond to trade. Dad thought it was a piece of glass; it was rectangular and it didn't sparkle. They took it to a jeweler in Munich who confirmed that not only was it real, but it was the finest quality diamond he had ever seen.

A few times Joe came to Munich to visit Dad at Yechiel's. One time Dad found a note from the landlady that Joe had called—he was in the hospital. He had been in a car accident and both his legs were broken.

The hospital was just ten minutes away and Dad went straight to see him. He found Joe with his legs bandaged and hoisted up in the air. Joe was crying, and when he saw Dad, he cried harder—what

Munich

would become of him—where would he go—he would be a cripple! Dad felt bad for him, he had Al, but Joe had nobody. Dad told him not to worry, "Where I sleep, you will sleep—what I eat, you will eat."

As it turned out, it wasn't as bad as Joe thought. He was released two weeks later, walking with the aid of crutches. He did stay with Dad in Icking, and when Dad went to study in Munich, Joe became friends with Mendel Dworski and stayed with him in Wolfratshausen. Later, Joe and Mendel both moved to Chicago where they remained life-long friends, although Mendel has since passed away. And Dad and Joe have always kept in touch.

At the end of 1947, Yechiel immigrated to South Africa. He had been corresponding with his two brothers there ever since the war ended. As a going away present, Dad and Al gave Yechiel the Luftwaffe camera. Yechiel told them that he'd send them the necessary paperwork so they could join him, although at the time Al was hot on moving to Eretz Yisrael, and it was all Dad could do to convince him to finish school. At the beginning Yechiel wrote to them every two weeks, which lasted for a while, but then tapered off. Dad and Al weren't the best correspondents either, but eventually they settled into a routine. Before each Rosh Hashanah Dad exchanged letters with Yechiel, and that lasted many, many years, well into the early 1990s. I even remember seeing some of those letters, not that I could read them since they were written in Yiddish.

When Dad was in Munich he used to stay with Yechiel, since he had two big beds in his room. After Yechiel left for Pretoria, Dad moved in with his brother on Baumgartnerstrasse. The first night Dad slept there, Al instructed him to leave his shoes outside the door. Dad was a bit confused and told Al that his shoes didn't smell—perhaps he meant his socks. Al told Dad not to spoil a good thing; the landlady polished his shoes when he left them outside the door. Dad thought Al was pulling his leg, but in the morning Dad's shoes shined like glass.

Al's landlady was thirty-two-years-old and had a son about six-years-old; her husband had been killed on the Russian front. To make extra money she rented out a room. She also had some relatives with a big farm and they constantly brought her food—salami, ham, cheese, butter, potatoes, onions and bread. Al and Dad paid her a little extra and she prepared dinner for them too. Her meals were delicious; they couldn't have eaten better in any restaurant at the time.

One night Al walked out of the room. Dad thought he went to the bathroom and had trouble falling asleep waiting for him to return. Al came back around six in the morning. Dad asked him, "What kind of sickness did you have that you couldn't find your way back to the room?" Al replied, "I had to take care of her, why do you think she treats us so well?"

One day the landlady's sixteen-year-old niece from the farm came for a visit. Dad was only four years older than her, yet she addressed him as "Mr. Pruchno." At the time Dad had his two-seater Mercedes convertible, and he asked permission to take the niece for a ride. He had a shipment of liquor to deliver and it would be nice to have the company. The landlady told Dad in no uncertain terms, her niece was a good Catholic girl, and if Dad wanted to fool around he better stick to girls his own age! Dad promised he would do nothing improper. He drove the niece around town with the top down; she was in heaven. He delivered the liquor, bought her an ice cream—and kissed her, but nothing more. Afterward she wrote to Dad a few times and always used the formal greeting, Mr. Pruchno.

Besides coffee and vehicles, Dad also did business in pianos. His friend Krotenberg introduced him to the owner of Winkler

Munich

Pianos. In 1948, after Israel became a state, many Jews leaving Germany wanted to take pianos with them. The government allowed them to take their furniture, which included pianos, without paying tariffs. Dad sold quite a few for $100-$120 each. (He received a discount for paying in advance.) He always had two in the hallway at any given time; the landlady didn't mind, he paid her extra for storage. Once Dad took her niece, who played very well, to the warehouse so she could advise him on which pianos had the best sound.

With pianos constantly coming and going, Dad came up with a plan. Yechiel had already moved to South Africa, yet Dad filled out the appropriate paperwork stating that Yechiel had left a baby grand behind, and he signed Yechiel's name. Dad went to Winkler's, and the owner himself played a seductive piece of music, Rimsky-Korsakov's *Scheherazade*, to aid Dad in his selection. Because Dad could only avoid paying the tariff once, Dad bought Yechiel the best piano available, a reconditioned Steinway. Dad bought it for $320, shipped it for $100, and Yechiel sold the piano to an English consul for $2000.

Dad's next car was a big convertible, a Wanderer, it was cheap enough to purchase, but it guzzled gasoline. Dad liked it—it had beautiful leather seats. As a precaution against theft, since it was a hassle to raise and lower the roof, Dad installed an ignition disconnect switch in a secret location. One day, Dad, Joe and Mendel drove to the Jewish Committee on Muhlstrasse in Munich. There was a lot of activity going on there, including trading on the black market. The area was also known as the hangout of the Jewish mafia. Dad parked on the street, activated the disconnect switch, and off they went to lunch.

When they returned the car was gone! Dad couldn't believe it. His first thought was that he had been sold a stolen car; the

Fall 1945 — Fall 1951

police had located it and towed it away. Dad called the police station, but no car matching its description had been found.

A moment later a man appeared, he was from the Jewish mafia, and he told Dad that he could have his car back in a couple of hours for the sum of one hundred dollars. Dad almost gave him the money, but then he thought better of it. Dad informed the man that the car did not belong to him, it belonged to the Irgun, and he demanded to speak with his superior right away.

The man departed for half an hour, and when he returned Dad went back with him. Dad wasted no time in telling him off. He asked the superior if he had ever heard of the Irgun (the militant Zionist group working to help establish a Jewish state in Eretz Yisrael). He continued that it wouldn't paint a pretty picture if he told their members in Munich what had happened to their car. The man apologized, claiming he was told the car belonged to a German. Dad thought—what a liar—no German would have come to that neighborhood. The man offered Dad lunch, which Dad refused, saying the Irgun had business to attend to, and he needed to get back immediately. All in all, the inconvenience took a couple of hours.

Al belonged to the Irgun, and although he never admitted it, Dad suspected. When certain visitors came to call, Al would tell Dad to disappear. One day Al introduced his visitors, who asked Dad if he knew where they could get ball bearings.

It took a few days, but Dad located the bearings through his German middleman, Kurt Lukovsky. They had to drive three hours from Munich to the factory to purchase them. The bearings were large and were placed in two wooden boxes in Dad's trunk. As he was moving the boxes, Kurt cut his hand, but he thought nothing of it.

By the time they were back on the road it was the middle of the night. Soon they were stopped by the German police and ordered to open their trunk. When the police saw blood on the boxes they accused Dad and Kurt of being black marketeers and transporting illegal meat. Even though they were shown the papers, the police insisted that the boxes be opened. The police were disappointed and reluctantly had to let Dad and Kurt go.

Dad sold the Wanderer; it was just too big. In its place he bought a Mercedes V170, which was dirt-cheap. He actually spotted it in a junkyard while on a train from Passau to Munich and went back to get it a couple of days later. The car was basically a disassembled carcass, but Dad knew an excellent mechanic and had it rebuilt. It looked as if it had just come out of the factory. He also had a radio installed, which he truly enjoyed, and it appealed to the German girls.

Dad was well on his way to becoming a playboy. On the weekdays, he was very busy with school and his various businesses, but on the weekends, he hung out with his friends and German shiksas (young, non-Jewish women). Generally, they had a good time; they went out to eat and to the movies. What they did afterward—I was told to use my imagination.

Dad went on a couple of dates with a Jewish girl from Fohrenwald. When Dad heard from her girlfriends that she was interested in him, and her parents were too—he ran away fast. At twenty years of age, Dad was not ready for marriage. A year later, Dad and Joe were standing by his car in Wolfratshausen, and this same girl asked them for a lift. Dad couldn't believe his eyes—she was married—and she was pregnant.

Dad not only had the cars, but the clothes as well. And whatever he bought for himself, he also bought for Al. One day Dad suggested that they go to the tailor together; they had often passed his shop in the center of town. They chose the fabrics, the same fabrics, and each had two suits made. In regards to clothing, Al deferred to Dad, since Dad really had a much better sense of style. They also bought the same shirts and shoes, but Dad insisted that they select their own ties. They wore their matching outfits, just like their Mother used to dress them when they were young.

When Al went on a date, Dad loaned him his car. When Al went on the class trip to Italy, Dad paid for the trip and gave him spending money. Dad also gave him money to buy them shirts and shoes. Al returned with silk shirts and leather shoes, again the same for both of them. Dad and Al only wore those handsome shirts twice, before a dry cleaner in Munich ruined them.

Dad always shared with Al—nobody was a better brother. As Dad said, "Anything I touched, I made money."

One Saturday, as Dad drove his Mercedes through the main section of Munich, the traffic was heavy and slow enough for him to notice a shiksa walking down the street, with a little dog on a leash running after her. From the back she looked very nice, and as Dad passed her, he turned his head to see that she was a very good-looking blonde. As she caught up to him, Dad lowered his window and said to her, "Have pity on your poor little dog, come, I'll drive you wherever you want to go." They spoke a bit, and she got in the car.

Dad suggested they stop for coffee and cake, or perhaps even a movie. Dad knew a nice little place (where Jews typically didn't go). It just so happened when they entered the establishment, Dad saw his neighbors, a Hungarian Jewish couple. Being single, Dad typically didn't have much to do with them, but when they saw Dad they motioned for him and his date to join them; Dad didn't really have a choice. The wife was unbelievably beautiful, but she had a terrible voice, and when she opened her mouth her beauty disappeared. They all had cake and coffee, but then Heidi, the shiksa, had to leave; the dog was not hers, but her landlady's. Dad drove her home and told her he would wait for her.

After ten minutes she came out wearing a red jacket. The jacket reminded Dad of a beautifully written story he had read in the ghetto by a Jewish writer named Sholem Asch. It was about a man who spent some years in prison, and when he was released he went crazy upon seeing a woman in a red dress, like a bull with a red cape. On some level Dad could relate.

Dad and Heidi spent quite a few hours together that day. Dad was a gentleman or at least played the part. He told himself it was a good idea to get involved with her; it was better to have one shiksa than ten. When I mistakenly referred to Heidi as his girlfriend, Dad reprimanded me, "How could she have been my girlfriend, she wasn't Jewish, she was my sex partner." Their relationship ended when Dad came to the States, but in the meantime, she accompanied him on quite a few business trips.

For many years there had been no legitimate economy in Europe. During the war, Dad had used the black market as a means of survival, and after the war, to make a living. But through Al's friend in the Irgun, Dad met some Jews from Austria, three brothers named Lifshitz, who elevated the use of the black market to a fine art. It became big business to smuggle coffee and cigarettes from Austria to Germany, where they could be sold for a hefty profit. At one point, the Brothers' market had grown to such an extent that they had bought out all the available coffee in Switzerland and then had to purchase their supply in Belgium.

After the war it was normal procedure for Germans to be returning from Austria with all their furniture and possessions. The Brothers employed an Austrian gentile who owned an unusual moving truck, with secret compartments and a double floor, accessed from beneath, where the contraband could be hidden. When the truck left the Austrian border, it was sealed by the Austrian authorities, and it could only be opened in Germany by the German authorities. But the ingenious truck allowed for the black market goods to be removed without tampering with the seal.

The Brothers asked Dad if he knew of a place where such a truck could be unloaded, with no prying eyes around. Near Yechiel's old room on the Kolner Platz, there was a German man, in his fifties, who owned a large garage where he kept his own truck. Dad went and spoke with him.

He was warm and easy-going, and he invited Dad to spend an evening in his home. His wife was French; they had been married before the war. He had been in the Wehrmacht and drove a truck, and the only thing he had wanted during the war, was to get out of it alive. His wife was good looking, but she had a hearing problem. Because Dad dressed nicely, she assumed he was French. Dad told her he wasn't, but she wouldn't hear of it. It was quite a conversation. She was so happy to have someone to talk to she didn't notice that she did all the talking. Dad mostly smiled, nodded and agreed "ya-ya, yo-yo."

The German and his wife had a daughter, rather ugly, but a good tennis player. She kept inviting Dad to watch her play, and Dad kept coming up with excuses. One day she wouldn't take no for an answer, after all she insisted, Dad did business with her father. Dad was surprised (and impressed) at how many people came to watch her match; afterward he was a mensch and took her out for dinner. It was Dad's good luck that she was away from home quite a bit, probably at the university.

Dad always used this German and his garage for the Brothers' black market jobs, and business flourished.

The Brothers concocted a credible scenario for transporting their goods as "care packages," utilizing an actual DP camp registry in order to obtain the Survivor's tax exemption.

The first time the Brothers sent Dad to make arrangements to ship these fake care packages from Switzerland to Feldafing, Dad was to replace a man who behaved too rudely to work out the deal. They didn't have to tell Dad twice to put on the charm, or to take Heidi along. Dad was less conspicuous at the Swiss/German border with a woman on his arm.

Heidi got ready in no time, and off they went to Lindau, about a three-hour drive from Munich. It was difficult to get a room overnight since they had no reservation, but Dad explained to the proprietor of the guesthouse that he would receive a generous tip if he helped Dad out. All of a sudden he was able to furnish them with a room.

When Dad awoke the next morning, he called the Chief Postmaster of the Region and spoke with his secretary. Dad apologized for calling on such short notice, but he just arrived from Switzerland, and his superiors insisted that it was of the utmost importance that Dad speak with the Postmaster without delay, for the welfare of young children was at stake. Dad was exceedingly courteous and accommodating, offering to take the Postmaster to lunch if his schedule was otherwise filled. Dad ingratiated himself to the secretary; if ever she came to Munich he would show her a good time. Dad heard her call out to her boss, "There's a man on the telephone from a Jewish agency—he's very polite..." Dad was told the Postmaster would see him in one hour. Dad was pleased. He dressed in a nice suit, and gave Heidi money to spend the day shopping; he would catch up with her later.

When Dad arrived, he thanked the secretary again and was escorted to the Postmaster's office. He thanked the Postmaster in person and then recited his carefully rehearsed script. Their agency organizes care packages to go to Jewish Survivors and their families in Feldafing. However, they were in need of transportation, specifically a truck large enough to hold approximately three thousand packages. They would gladly pay for use of such a truck, they just had to make it happen quickly, otherwise the packages would spoil sitting in the warehouse. Dad was sweet as sugar, and the Postmaster gave him everything he wanted. The "care packages" of coffee, tea, cigarettes and chocolate made it to the black market as scheduled.

The Brothers employed this pretense a few times, but in no way did they jeopardize the Survivor's receipt of any actual care packages.

The Brothers were religious people. When they ate out, they went to the only kosher restaurant in Munich, but mostly they brought food with them from home. They came to Munich on Sunday evenings and returned home to Linz (Austria) on Thursday evenings; they wanted to be with their wives for Shabbat. Quite a few times Dad drove them in his Mercedes to the border, and from there they would take a streetcar or taxi. One Shabbat Dad spent with them, but it was a hassle, he had to get a special travel permit.

Dad ate at the kosher restaurant quite frequently. Because no business transactions occurred on Shabbat, Dad enjoyed dinner on Friday or lunch on Saturday when he paid in advance. It was owned by a couple named Adele and Henry Goldbloom. Remarkably, their daughter, Rose Newman, is one of the congregants at the shul Dad currently attends, Young Israel of Southfield.

Since Dad chauffeured the Brothers often, he heard a lot about their business propositions, but being so young, in his early twenties, he mostly just listened. One day they were talking about a fantastic plan, proposed by an Austrian journalist, to resuscitate the city of Lindau, which could no longer afford to pay for its public services. The Mayor of Lindau agreed to permit two large truckloads of coffee, supplied by the Brothers, to enter the city. The first would be sold on the open market to German importers. That coffee would be heavily taxed to help offset the city's financial obligations. The Brothers, however, would cover their expenses and make their money on the second truckload of coffee, which would be sold on the black market.

Later that same day, Kurt Lukovsky paid Dad a visit. He would drop by from time to time to see if Dad had any work for him, since he was starting up his own import/export business. Dad questioned him about the big name coffee importers in Germany. Kurt explained that before the war there was a big importer in Hamburg and another in Frankfurt, each had their own fleet of trucks and packaging facilities. After all, what did Dad really know about coffee?

The following day the Brothers were furious. The Polish Jew they had negotiated with couldn't meet their deadline; the deal would have to be postponed, and that would cost them a lot of money. As usual they were discussing the situation in front of Dad. But this time Dad spoke up. He mentioned that he had heard (from Kurt) that another big coffee importer, from Hanover, was in town for the week vacationing with his wife, and if they wanted, Dad would go talk with him, "to see what would develop."

As it turned out, the Hanover importer was interested in doing business. He said Germany was a big country and it hadn't had any real coffee for years. Not only during the war, but for some time afterward, the government had not allowed the importing of coffee, which was considered a luxury item.

Dad was anxious that the quantities might be too great for the importer to handle, but he assured Dad that he was prepared to buy any amount of coffee Dad had to sell. The importer had other concerns, mainly that the documentation for the customs official was indeed genuine. Dad tried to reassure him, yet at the same time warn him, not to show the customs official the papers unnecessarily. (Once the papers were signed—sometimes they were and sometimes they weren't—they couldn't be used again, and the papers were needed for both shipments of coffee.) Dad concluded their meeting by informing the importer that he would need to pay in cash. The importer was wary; this kind of money was always transferred by check. Dad replied that he was just the middleman, that his people in Switzerland required cash, or there was no deal. Ultimately the importer agreed to the terms.

The next afternoon Dad and Kurt drove in Dad's Mercedes to meet the coffee truck at a warehouse in Munich selected by the importer. The driver of the truck had the original papers and Dad had a copy. The importer was already there, holding a briefcase.

They walked up to greet him, and Dad just about fainted as the importer introduced him to the customs official. Immediately Dad realized that had he been in the importer's shoes he would have done the exact same thing. The importer had laid out too large a sum of money for the documentation not to be legitimate. Dad stayed cool and calm as the official took a few minutes to look over the papers and declare everything in order. Once he left, they started unloading the coffee.

The importer opened a couple of bags at random, and he smelled the beans to make sure they weren't spoiled. Only then did he give Dad the money, a briefcase full, which Dad counted right then and there.

This arrangement with the double shipments of coffee, one taxed and the other untaxed (black market), went on for a few months. Dad orchestrated everything so beautifully it ran like clockwork, and the Brothers made a lot of money. However, Dad was wondering when he would get paid; typically they paid him often, and very well. Finally, after three months, they gave him a large sum of money, five thousand dollars. They thought Dad

Munich

was a genius. In the end Dad worked for the Brothers, on and off, for about nine months.

Besides the Hanover importer, Dad made quite an impression on the Hamburg importer as well. He just couldn't believe the way Dad conducted himself in business at the tender age of twenty-two, and he wished his son could be more like him.

Via telephone, the Hamburg importer introduced Dad to the Frankfurt importer, describing his colleague as an even bigger dealer than he was. Dad asked the Frankfurt importer if he wanted to buy some coffee; he would have a big truckload available that Friday.

The Frankfurt importer was interested, and already knew he would have to pay in cash. But for one reason or another Dad didn't trust him. He wondered how he could get his trucks from Frankfurt to Lindau in such a short time; they'd have to drive all night. So instead Dad turned around and sold the Frankfurter's coffee to the importer from Hamburg.

Late that Friday afternoon, as Dad and the Hamburg importer sat talking and enjoying a coffee on the terrace of the most lavish hotel in Lindau, who should stroll toward them, but the Frankfurt importer. Dad knew it was him because he walked with a wobble, one leg being shorter than the other. Dad felt awful, what was he going to do? There were no plausible excuses, so he simply told the truth.

Dad admitted to the Hamburg importer that he didn't think the Frankfurt importer would show up. He asked if it would be possible to take back half the coffee and make it up the following week. The Hamburg importer was agreeable.

Then Dad confessed to the Frankfurt importer, who angrily responded that if he had promised to be there, he would be there. Then he calmed down and said that he hoped they could do more business together in the future. Dad liked how he had solved the problem, instinctively putting his Father's words into action—be honest.

The Frankfurt importer went into the warehouse to check on his half of the coffee. He found it acceptable. It wasn't the best grade of beans, but it was at least average or above. That evening at dinner they talked a lot about coffee; where the best beans were grown, how harvesting can affect the beans, and how shipping by boat can spoil the beans. Dad received quite an education and suggested that he go to Columbia to import the beans himself. The importer quickly discouraged Dad; financially, it was much too risky a proposition.

Not all transactions ended profitably. The man who introduced Dad and the Lifshitz Brothers, a friend of Al's, knew an Austrian customs inspector who could be bribed. The inspector would provide the seal on a truckload of cigarettes (two million of them) to be sold on the black market in Germany. For some reason Dad could not make the initial meeting with the inspector in Fuessen, so he sent Al in his place, and in his car.

A week later Dad and Al's friend went to "meet" the truck. They parked some distance away hoping to see, with the aid of binoculars, the truck sail through customs and across the border. They would follow at a distance, all the way to the Kolner Platz garage in Munich. Instead they saw the police unloading and searching the truck. The customs inspector had betrayed them. Quickly they jumped in Dad's car and sped away.

The next day Dad received a message to come in for questioning. Dad doesn't understand exactly how the police identified him; it had something to do with a notebook that had fallen from his car.

Dad spent the next few weeks in the Landsberg prison. He joked with Al that Hitler wrote *Mein Kampf* from that prison, maybe he should write a book too. Six hours a day Dad sawed firewood. He was fed well and allowed visitors. Al brought him "good stuff," including cigarettes, some of which he gave to the guards, "Take them, I won't tell anyone."

I asked Dad if he was scared or worried. His reply, "No, not really." By comparison life in prison was much better than life in a concentration camp. Besides, the maximum penalty for a customs violation was only a couple of years.

A newspaper clipping describing the trial, which Dad had saved all these years and recently uncovered in his mess of an office, stated, "The customs agency had however significantly underestimated Samuel. He appeared at the proceedings not only with panache but also a good lawyer." (Interestingly, they never used Dad's last name in the article.)

The lawyer advised that Dad and Al come to the trial dressed the same. That was not a problem considering Dad always bought them the same suits. When the lawyer questioned the customs inspector and another witness as to which of the two brothers they had seen at the initial meeting in Fuessen, one witness said it was Al, and the other said it was neither, the man he remembered was bigger than either of them. (Al was in fact a couple of inches shorter than Dad.) Dad remembers one of them saying, "They look alike."

The judge dismissed the case. Dad even received a small sum of money as compensation for being falsely accused. The Brothers, however, lost quite a bit of money on that business deal.

At about this time a great calamity befell Dad. His beautiful, thick, wavy, brown hair started coming out in clumps in the shower. He ran from one doctor to another. Finally he decided it was a skin problem and sought out the most renowned specialist in the city. The doctor smiled at Dad, and asked if Dad's Father was bald. The doctor had the same problem, and pointing to his own head said, "If you don't want to lose your hair, then put it in a box." He told Dad not to waste his time and money, and he didn't charge him for the visit.

However, Dad wasn't satisfied quite yet. He found a foreign doctor who advised treatment three times a week for three hundred dollars. Dad's major concern was the time it would take; between school and work he was a very busy man. So he made the doctor an offer. If he cured him, Dad would give him twice the amount, if not, he'd give him nothing. The doctor declined Dad's offer, and that was the end of Dad's search. But he gave one more suggestion, albeit a superstition, a try. He shaved his head in the hope it would grow back twice as thick—needless to say, it didn't. In the end it took about two years until Dad was sporting the hairstyle he would have for life.

When I was a little girl, I asked Mom what color Dad's hair was; she told me to go and take a look. I came back exclaiming, "He has no hair!"

On occasion Dad stayed at the luxurious hotel in Lindau. The first time he was there with Kurt, and they were dining with the importers and their wives—an experience fit for a king, and the food was exceptional. Dad looked at the table and saw multiple plates, forks, knives, spoons and glasses. He didn't want to appear uncouth in front of the importers, so he whispered to Kurt, "What's with all the cutlery?" Kurt response was simply to follow his lead. I can just picture that scene as if from an old-time movie—dashingly handsome young man, out of his element...think Laurence Olivier in *Wuthering Heights*.

Another time in Lindau, Dad and Kurt walked into a Mercedes dealership. There was a brand new 1949 sedan, a real beauty, in black with wine colored upholstery. The price was

$2100, and there was a six month wait, or longer. Dad wanted that car so badly he told the salesman he would give him an extra hundred dollars if he could drive it out of the showroom that day. The salesman went to speak with his boss, and Dad overheard something about "a crazy foreigner." Nevertheless, the boss let Dad have the car. Dad felt as if he had just made history, offering more than the sticker price.

Dad bought a lot of accessories for his new car—fog lights, special back up lights, side lights, search lights and a police-like siren, just in case he had a problem. Dad took extra special care of that car, it was his first new car, the only thing he actually owned, and he was very proud of it.

Dad gave his old Mercedes, the V170, to Kurt, who couldn't have been happier. Dad owed him a little money and wanted to do something special for him, since he was always so helpful. Whether it involved obtaining information, or closing a deal when Dad's foreign accent would prove a hindrance, he could always depend on Kurt.

One day Dad drove the Brothers in his new Mercedes to the Austrian border. On his way back to Munich he was enjoying the drive on the Autobahn; the sun was setting, the scenery was beautiful, and music was playing on the radio. Before long, he came upon two American soldiers standing on the side of the road and they were waving for him to stop. Dad was happy to give them a ride—why should American soldiers, who liberated him, wait in the cool evening air? They offered Dad a cigarette, which he accepted.

When they were about twenty minutes from Munich, Dad heard one say to the other, let's throw him out and take the car, pick up some girls and have a good time. Dad became nervous; he knew they weren't joking around. But always quick on his feet, Dad turned on the additional lights and the siren. He stopped at the outskirts of Munich and told the soldiers that the car belonged to the Munich chief of police and he was running late, they would have to catch the streetcar the rest of the way. The soldiers obviously thought it better not to mess with the police chief, and they got out of the car. Dad was relieved and never picked up another soldier again.

Yechiel came to visit Dad and Al in Munich in the fall of 1948, after first stopping in Israel. He wrote to them that he would let them know when he was due to arrive, but he never did. He came to Munich on a Saturday afternoon and went straight to their room. He introduced himself to the landlady who knew of him from his letters; Dad had given her son the stamps. She told Yechiel he could find Dad at Heidi's apartment. Let's just say Dad was a bit embarrassed, but he recovered and dressed quickly, and off they went to a coffee house.

Yechiel spent a week in Munich, staying at a hotel on a side street not far from the Kolner Platz, in his old neighborhood. Dad, Al and Yechiel went out to eat every lunch and dinner; most of the time Dad paid. They were like the "Three Musketeers." When Yechiel needed to exchange pounds for marks, they all took a trip to the bank. They were nicely dressed in suits and ties; Dad and Al with their dark hair, Yechiel with his moustache, they looked like gangsters.

As soon as they walked in, the teller got nervous and buzzed the manager. Dad conceded it must have looked a little strange, three men walking into a bank and only one of them conducting business. Soon the police arrived, under the pretense of conducting their own banking business. What did they think this was going to be—a holdup? Yechiel told the manager he was an English citizen, and they should learn to be more polite to foreigners. Dad and Al kept their mouths shut.

In the evenings they went to the movies and saw friends; they talked about Israel. Having just been there, Yechiel had first hand knowledge. He told them the economy was very bad; there were no jobs to be had. Educated people from their city, engineers and accountants, were driving taxis and having a hard time making a living. Yechiel asked what they would do there—live on a kibbutz? (They weren't the type to live on a communal settlement in the countryside.) Yechiel insisted that Dad and Al fill out immigration papers to South Africa, and if conditions improved, then they could reconsider Israel. Dad had known Yechiel since he was ten-years-old—he looked up to him. It didn't matter what Dad had been through, or what he had accomplished, he still felt Yechiel knew what was best for him, and for his brother.

Dad drove Yechiel to the airport. He was continuing on to London. He wanted to purchase property there, and not only for investment purposes. Should he ever have to flee South Africa, he would have somewhere to go; that was the lesson he had learned from the war.

When the small plane took off, Dad waved, and he wondered if he would ever see Yechiel again. Dad knew he would remarry—but a man can't forget his past, can he? Yechiel did remarry, in Johannesburg in 1949 to a girl from Shavl named Pescia. He sent Dad and Al a letter with a picture of him and his new wife. In 1950 Yechiel and Pescia came to visit them for a few days on their way home from London.

I met Yechiel only twice in my life. The first time he visited I was very young, about four-years-old. Dad and Yechiel were in our basement rec room talking, and Mom was puttering around the kitchen. I was running up and down the stairs between them, all dressed up for the occasion, wearing a party dress and my brand new, black, patent leather shoes. I slipped on the uncarpeted stairs and somersaulted all the way down. I probably wouldn't have remembered his visit at all except that it was the backdrop for my spectacular fall.

Fall 1945 — Fall 1951

The second visit was a bit later. I was in my late teens, and Yechiel came with Pescia and their two sons, Sayra—the friendly, and Avigdor—the handsome. I remember it being a very enjoyable visit.

Twenty years passed and I received a phone call from Yechiel in South Africa. It was during Pesach and he was trying to get in touch with Dad, but Dad and Judy were away. He wanted to tell Dad that his wife had passed away. He told me that he had instructed his sons to never lose track of the Pruchnos, "They are good people and the best family you will ever have."

A few years later Yechiel died, and his sons and their families moved to Australia. I wrote to them, they wrote back, and then we exchanged our dads' Spielberg tapes. As Dad, Judy, my husband Eli, and I watched his testimony, we were dumbfounded. Yechiel never mentioned that he was married to Dad's sister, or that he survived the war side by side with Dad and Al. They received no more than a passing reference as "the Pruchno Brothers." Yet while watching Dad's tape (and reading his story), Yechiel was a prominent figure. Dad had treated Yechiel like a brother. Dad even joked that his Mother had treated her son-in-law better than either of her sons. And in Dachau, Yechiel had chosen to stay with them over his own brother.

Yechiel's tape changed Dad's heart—he felt betrayed. He was glad Al didn't live to see it; as it was he would roll over in his grave. At some point Dad had called Yechiel in South Africa, and Yechiel told him how sick he was; he had cancer. Dad felt like getting on a plane and going to see him, just to see if he still cared for Yechiel after all these years. But Yechiel talked him out of it, saying it was a long way to go for such a short visit. Yechiel died soon after. In hindsight, Dad was glad he didn't go; he would have felt betrayed twice.

In 1951 Dad and Al were deliberating over where they should go. Dad was twenty-four-years-old, and Al was twenty-eight. They both had their diplomas. Dad felt it was time to leave Germany, as conventional economies were improving, the black market business was drying up. Many years later a rumor circulated through the family that Dad had to leave Germany, because of some business dealings that had gone awry, but Dad steadfastly denies it. He simply felt his life as a playboy wasn't normal, and he didn't like the man he saw in the mirror every morning. He wanted to settle down and build a future.

South Africa had refused them twice, and once they even had Yechiel's help in filling out the paperwork. Their choice was either Israel or the United States. Dad kept hearing Yechiel's voice in his head about life in the Jewish state, and he had no desire to live on a kibbutz. They had no relatives in Israel, or very close friends. (Only Feivel Krotenberg moved there, and he kept sending Dad letters urging him come.) Dad preferred the idea of trying life in the States, and if they didn't like it, they could pack up their few suitcases and go to Israel. Al agreed. In preparation they took private English lessons. They filled out the papers, and in three months they were approved to go to the United States. They chose Detroit, with the growing automotive industry they thought they would easily get jobs.

For a man traveling light, just two suitcases, Dad packed some interesting items.

He had done some business in carbide inserts with a man from Bad Reichenhall, but the man didn't have any cash, and Dad wanted to get paid before he left Germany. It would have been far easier to travel with coins or stamps, but instead the man gave Dad a dozen or so small paintings of undetermined value, which of course, Dad shared with Al. Dad's intention was to sell the paintings when he got to the States, but no one wanted to buy them. Later, when Al got married, he proposed that Dad give him all the paintings, and then when Dad got married he'd give him back half. Dad thought—how could he take them back after they've been hanging on his sister-in-laws walls? He decided he was better off keeping his own paintings.

In Dad's pocket was a brass keychain of a monkey's face with his arms encircling a disc. The words, in German, were only discernable when the disc was spun, and they read, "Leck mich am Arsch." In other words, "Kiss my Ass." I was a child when I discovered it in Dad's drawer and took it as my own, although I never used it, for fear I'd lose it.

Dad brought his Leica, the camera he had bought himself to replace Yechiel's good-bye present, and the photographs he had taken with it. I remember that Leica, and having to pose, for what seemed like an eternity, as he carefully focused each shot. Al borrowed it once when he and his wife went to Florida. He accidentally dropped it in the ocean, and it was never the same again.

Right before Dad boarded the ship to the States, he walked into a store and bought, with the last of his German marks, a chess set of intricate medieval figurines. While I was growing up, Dad never had time to play chess, so the set sat boxed and put away. I had no idea he was such an accomplished player. Now he spends Shabbat afternoons playing with a neighbor, a registered player, and their games typically end in a draw, hours later. And his elaborate chess set currently sits in my living room, waiting for someone to play it, but at least it is on display, not far from my candlesticks.

Dad left behind the last car he owned in Germany—the BMW 328 roadster. It was built before the war in 1939 and it was an awesome car, a real head turner. It was a convertible with six cylinders and three carburetors, and it sat low to the ground. Dad had it for about a year, and when he drove by people looked at him as though he were the King of Bavaria.

Many years later an acquaintance gave Dad an article about that car. There had been only 464 of them built between 1936

Munich

and 1940, and currently they are worth a quarter-million dollars each. Dad had sold his for $2000. If only he had that car now!

Since the end of the war, countless Lithuanians and their families had immigrated to the United States, pretending to be displaced persons, claiming to have been forced by the Nazis to come to Germany. The United States government did not distinguish between the Lithuanian collaborators and their Jewish victims; all were welcome under the Displaced Persons Act.

Fall 1945 — Fall 1951

Al, Yechiel Saks and Dad
the Pruchno brothers and their brother-in-law.

Al, Dad and Yechiel
the "Three Musketeers."

149

Munich

Dad and Al
in their matching suits, shirts and shoes, but different ties.

Dad
as bathing beauty.

Dad and Yechiel
before his brother-in-law left for South Africa.

Fall 1945 — Fall 1951

Dad
in the Wanderer.

Al
with the famed BMW.

151

ATLANTIC OCEAN

✭ ✭ ✭

FALL 1951

The Pruchno brothers arrived in the United States on the *USS General R. M. Blatchford* in November 1951. It was arranged through UNRRA, the United Nations Relief and Rehabilitation Administration, and a Jewish agency that paid for their passage. The ship departed from Bremerhaven, and as it moved away from port, Dad and Al got their last glimpses of Germany. At long last Dad let his true feelings emerge, "What a beautiful sight it would be to see Germany burn now."

The ship was not a luxury ship, but a liberty ship, built quick and cheap to transport soldiers in WWII. Everything was for communal use, needless to say, it was not the cleanest. The passengers slept where the soldiers had slept, on a lower deck, not in cabins but in dormitories, swinging from hammocks. Meals were served on an upper deck. The first evening they ate hotdogs and beans, which Dad always liked, if there were leftovers they could have seconds. A few people on the ship were even from their hometown of Shavl.

Once the ship came to the English Channel, the water got rough, the weather rainy and miserable. Most of the passengers became seasick. Dad felt like throwing up all the time and couldn't decide whether it was better to eat or not. They walked around the deck in the foul weather, with paper bags in hand (just in case), but the fresh air felt good.

One mealtime, as Dad and Al were standing in line behind a rope waiting to go into the mess hall, Dad noticed a Jewish

Atlantic Ocean

woman and her two small children in front of them. The children were restless and went on the other side of the rope, and when their mother went to get them an UNRRA officer pushed her. If Dad hadn't caught her, she would have fallen to the floor. Dad grabbed the UNRRA officer by his lapels, he was very close to punching him in the face, and yelled, "Never push a woman in my presence again, I saw that too many times in Germany!" Nearby, people were looking on and murmuring their agreement.

Admittedly, Dad went a little overboard, but in his mind, the woman (who he never did see again), could have been his sister. The UNRRA officer said he would not allow Dad and Al to enter the United States, and for the second half of the four-day voyage Dad worried about being sent back to Germany.

When they arrived at the Port of New York, it was very early in the morning. In the darkness they could see roads delineated with car headlights and the Statue of Liberty; it was a magnificent view. The passengers were lined up to go to shore, collect their suitcases, and go through inspection. The Captain was present, along with some other officers and the UNRRA officer. The UNRRA officer told Dad and Al to stand aside. Dad was sure he was going to be sent back to Germany, but maybe they would let his brother continue on.

When all the passengers, and even some crew, had disembarked, the Captain asked why those two men had been singled out. The UNRRA officer explained that they wouldn't make very good citizens; they didn't behave themselves and should be sent back. The Captain looked at Dad and Al, and then he asked them what had happened. Dad explained in his very best broken English, and to his surprise, the Captain just let them go.

As Dad later pointed out, "What a wise man the Captain was, between Al and me, we paid enough in taxes to buy not one, but two liberty ships."

Fall 1951

Dad
on the USS General R.M. Blatchford *leaving Germany—1951.*

DETROIT

✫ ✫ ✫

FALL 1951 — LATE 1960S

Dad and Al felt good to be standing on solid ground; their nauseousness disappeared. They were picked up by a young woman from HIAS, the Hebrew Immigrant Aid Society. She was very nice and polite, although Dad was a little thrown by her attire; she wore saddle shoes. Dad had only seen nurses wear such shoes. Dad and Al, of course, were dressed in the height of European fashion. They put their luggage in storage; their train to Detroit wasn't scheduled to depart until eight o'clock that evening.

In the meantime, the young woman took them to a cafeteria for an early dinner. They had never seen anything like it before, so she explained that they could choose whatever they wanted. Picking up a tray, Dad was quickly inundated with decisions. Even an item as simple as bread became complicated; did he want dark bread, light bread, white bread or buns? Then there were the potatoes—white potatoes, red potatoes or sweet potatoes, with gravy or without—let alone the entrée to select. And the people kept piling up behind him. It was enough to make him lose his appetite.

The woman paid for their meals, and finally they sat down to eat. Afterward she suggested they go for a walk, since they had quite a few hours until their departure. Munich was a big city, but nothing compared to New York, with its towering buildings, monumental bridges, and trains running above and below ground. Dad found this just as mind-boggling in person as when

Detroit

his Father had first described them, so long ago. And then there was the traffic. The sidewalks were crowded with people pushing and shoving; there was no politeness.

Dad walked behind Al and the young woman, since there wasn't room enough to walk three abreast. Besides, he was too overwhelmed to speak. He was quite relieved when she said it was time to go to the train. She drove them to collect their bags and then to the station, where she purchased their tickets and brought them to the platform. Dad thought it would be a long, long time before he came back to New York, New York.

Once in their compartment they got comfortable, removing their coats, hats and ties, and they settled in for the twelve-hour ride to Detroit. When the train started moving, they fell asleep. Dad awoke in the middle of the night and stared out the window. He remembered many nights walking out of nightclubs at five in the morning, getting into his car, and driving home. What kind of life was that? What was in store for him next? He resolved that he would do his best and "see what would develop."

When Dad and Al arrived in Detroit, a young Jewish couple (also from HIAS) approached them, introduced themselves, and took them to breakfast. While they waited for their food, the couple told them what to expect. Al mentioned he had just finished college in Munich, and would look for a job as an engineer; Dad added he would look for work as a toolmaker. The man was more accommodating than his wife. As he started to give them his address, in case they needed any help, she elbowed him in the ribs. What was she worried about—that they would bother them for every little thing? Whenever Dad and Al recalled that day, they would laugh thinking she must have broken a rib.

The couple drove them to a four-unit flat, about forty minutes away, in a Jewish neighborhood of Detroit, around Dexter and Livernois, where HIAS had arranged a room for them in the apartment of an older Jewish couple. The man worked on the assembly line at Ford, and they were both as nice as could be. HIAS had even paid for their lodging for the first two or three months, until they got on their feet.

The room was small, especially after they brought in their four suitcases. After they unpacked and hung up their clothing, they found themselves in an awkward position. The woman had phoned a neighbor to come and look at their beautiful, tailor made, European clothes.

That evening Dad and Al went out for dinner to a restaurant that catered to the tastes of Jews from the old country, serving chicken soup with kreplach, gefilte fish, etc. Although it wasn't too expensive, it didn't take Dad long to realize that they couldn't afford to eat out breakfast, lunch and dinner; he only had about a thousand dollars.

When they returned home, Dad saw, for the first time ever, a small black and white television. They watched the comedian Milton Berle. Although the reception wasn't great, their landlord was always glued to the TV.

This is where the Pruchno brothers began their American lives.

Within a couple of days, Dad and Al took their first trip downtown to Jewish Family Services; they were required to go weekly for a certain period of time. When they got on the bus, Dad didn't bother sitting down, he just figured he'd have to get up again when an older woman got on. So they stood and looked around. Soon two Jewish girls got on and stood next to them. It was hard to communicate, but Dad could swear the girls were trying to pick them up.

One day after they left JFS, approaching from the opposite direction as they crossed Woodward Avenue, was an old friend of Al's. The two men embraced and kissed, as if finding a long lost

Detroit

brother. Dad was confused; he didn't remember Abrasha Pesis. Abrasha was overjoyed to see them. He was on his lunch hour and took them for coffee; he worked nearby at a clothing store. He was a tailor, who occasionally doubled as a salesman, so he was nicely dressed, "American" style. He insisted that they come to his house for dinner that very evening.

As it turned out they lived near each other, only a fifteen-minute walk between them. Abrasha was married to a woman named Gruna; they had been married back in Lithuania. They had a baby boy named Jacob. (Later they would have another boy, Solomon.) Gruna was so beautiful when Dad met her; that to this day he never fails to mention it when he speaks of her.

Dad and Al were always welcome at the Pesis' home and spent many evenings there. Gruna was a good cook and always had food for them. She was warm and generous. She even insisted they bring their washing to her; it wasn't a problem, she would just put it in the machine, and it would wash itself. Dad was a bit concerned about imposing so much, since the Pesis didn't have much money either, but Al said not to worry, they'd make it up to them later.

A few times Dad and Al offered to baby-sit. Gruna would put Jack to sleep before they left, but invariably, he would wake up inconsolable. Clueless, Dad and Al would spend the night taking turns holding and rocking him.

Dad once asked Abrasha why he and Gruna were so nice to them. Abrasha replied that Al had been very nice to him when he had come to Shavl from Poland after the German invasion. Al had taken him under his wing and into his crowd of friends.

Abrasha took them to the store where he worked and insisted they buy new clothes, so they wouldn't have "greener" written all over them. (Greener—an American Yiddish expression for someone who has just come off the boat and is not yet accustomed to American ways.) Actually that was how Abrasha happened to notice them that day across Woodward Avenue. Dad thought

Fall 1951 — Late 1960s

their clothes were beautiful, and they were practically brand new. Dad and Al had purposefully bought new clothes before they left Germany because they didn't know when they'd be able to afford to do so again. After they made some money, they reluctantly agreed with Abrasha and purchased some new clothes. However, the shoes Dad couldn't part with, he still had some of them years later when he married Mom.

Abrasha and Gruna were known to the next generation as Uncle Albert and Aunt Gloria. Uncle Albert was a kind and gentle man, I adored him, and I think he felt the same way about me. He died during my first year of college. Aunt Gloria passed away while nearing completion of this book. The last time I saw her, she was still baking the same treats she did when I was a little girl, scone-like chocolate chip cookies and kichel.

Aunt Gloria was a strong woman, a real character. She had to be to endure leaving her daughter Francis (from an earlier marriage) behind in Russia and not being able to get her out until she was a teenager.

She was also one of the most opinionated people I ever knew. In her unusually high voice, she once told me that she understood my going to college, it was a good place to shop for a husband, but why go to graduate school, did I want to be smarter than my husband?

Aunt Gloria also told me that Dad was so comfortable in their home that he would take off his pants and sit in his gatkes (underpants), just so his pants wouldn't wrinkle before going out on a date.

Gruna introduced Dad and Al to some of her cousins; one was Joe Orley, a man well known in the Jewish community. Joe owned a factory in Dearborn that built refrigerators, and he gave Dad and Al their first jobs in January 1952, a couple of months after their arrival. Al worked there as a designer and stayed on one-and-a-half years. Then he worked at Willys-Overland Motors, but ultimately he spent the majority of his career as an engineer at Ford Motor Co.

Dad worked at Orleys for only three months and quit. Dad's foreman was a German, who kept lamenting the fact that his son was serving in Korea when he could really use his considerable tool making expertise. Dad felt this foreman wasn't doing a good job for the Orleys. He had no idea how to utilize Dad's abilities, and he sold the Orleys a bunch of machines so old they belonged in a museum.

Before starting at Orleys, Dad and Al had looked in the newspapers and saw many listings for toolmakers, machinists and operators. They chose a place not far from where they lived and went to apply for a job. They happened to walk into the lobby just as the owner did. They explained to him that they were looking for work, having just come from Germany a month ago, and although their English wasn't the best, they were skilled. The owner asked them a few questions about Europe, but nothing related to employment. When Al asked if he could use the "toilet," the owner corrected him saying "bathroom or restroom." Then the owner made a statement that hit Dad and Al like a brick—he said he would never hire Jews; they don't like to work with their hands, they only like to "do business." Dad and Al were stunned. Coming from Europe the last thing they expected to hear was a Jew refusing to hire someone because he was Jewish. Dad and Al would have done anything to get their feet in the door—they would have cleaned the shop.

After being in the motor capital of the world for a few months, Dad and Al realized they would need to buy a car. Dad had two thousand dollars in savings, which he had given to Yechiel for both himself and his brother, and they wrote to Yechiel for their money.

On one of Yechiel's visits to Germany, they had discussed the safest way to get American dollars out. Because Yechiel was on his way to England, he could deposit their money there, and in just a few days he could transfer it anywhere. In actuality it took about three months, but Yechiel transferred the money to their new savings account in Detroit, in three installments, without interest.

Dad and Al then went to a car dealership on Jefferson Avenue and bought a new Chevrolet Bel Air for $2200. It was a nice car, and it had a radio. Dad drove; Al may have been the automotive engineer, but Dad was the better driver.

One day Dad came home to find a notice. He needed to register with Selective Services for the Army. Dad was the right age—lucky for Al, he was already too old. Dad was quite upset; he wasn't even a citizen yet. He was afraid he would be drafted into the American army and shipped back to Germany. He should have gone to Israel!

A week later he went downtown to the recruiting office, filled out the paperwork, and had the medical examination. A month later he received another notice. He wasn't being called up—but his name was now on file.

That obstacle behind him, Dad started searching for a job in earnest. He filled out applications on the west side of the city, where he lived, and on the east side too. Prospective employers wanted to know how much experience he had. Dad was twenty-five-years-old, how much experience could he have had? Everybody was looking for twelve to fifteen years; he had two to three years at best.

Detroit

Three weeks after Dad left Orleys he found another job. Dad saw a nice machine shop on Eight Mile Road and Groesbeck Highway, Huber Tool and Die. Even today, whenever he drives past the building, he is filled with fond memories.

Dad walked into the employment office, filled out an application, and the secretary called in the superintendent. Dad greeted him with a cheerful good morning, and as soon as he replied Dad knew he was a German. Dad told the superintendent about himself and showed him his diploma. He gave Dad a slip of paper to go to the clinic down the street for a medical exam, without which he couldn't be hired. Dad walked over, had the exam, and got the report in a sealed envelope. He walked back and handed it to the superintendent, who commented that Dad must be really anxious to go to work. He started mid-week. It always struck Dad as ironic that a Jew wouldn't hire him, but a German did.

The owner of Huber Tool and Die was a German engineer who had come to the United States before the First World War. Many of the workers were Americans of German descent, but there were also a fair number who came from Germany in the early 1950s, straight to the factory with their suitcases in hand. In the lunchroom they spoke German and talked a lot about WWII. Dad's German was good, although he spoke with an accent.

One day his co-workers asked him which branch of the military he was in during the war. Dad replied that he wasn't in the military; he had been in a concentration camp. They didn't understand what Dad was talking about, or they didn't want to. They asked him this question repeatedly, and one day Dad answered differently.

He was reading a book about Field Marshall Rommel, so he said he had been in the Afrika Korps. That answer they liked. Then one German asked if he remembered how cold it was at night. And Dad knowledgably agreed—it was hot during the day, but as soon as the sun went down it got very cold.

Fall 1951 — Late 1960s

Only once did Dad have a small problem with a co-worker, and this occurred on his very first day. Naturally, he got to work early, and he inadvertently took the parking space of a man who had been working there for twenty years. From then on Dad simply parked further away.

Basically Dad was liked. He did a good job and worked a lot of overtime, which gave him his much-needed experience.

Just before Thanksgiving, about a year after Dad and Al arrived in the States, their first cousin, George Zak from Cleveland, contacted them. George's son Michael relayed the following story. One day back in 1951, his father had gone for his customary haircut, but his regular barber wasn't in. Instead, he took a cut from a barber "fresh off the boat," originally from Shavl. George and the barber spoke, while Michael and his brother Allen amused themselves. Michael wasn't sure what they were talking about (he didn't speak Yiddish), but he knew it was important when the shop got unnaturally quiet.

George had been bemoaning that his cousins, the Pruchnos, had perished during the war. The barber quickly corrected him—he was with Dad and Al on the day they were liberated, and the last he had heard they were living in Germany. It didn't take long for George to contact Jewish Family Services, but it took JFS over a year to locate the brothers, first in Munich, and eventually in Detroit.

I never tire of hearing Michael talk about the day Dad and Al came to Cleveland for a visit—the anticipation was palpable. Michael was twelve at the time and his mother, Terri, told him to go to the window and keep watch for them. Michael wondered how he was supposed to know who they were. His mother replied, "They'll be the good-looking ones."

Michael expected to meet two guys down on their luck, however, the men who walked through their front door were anything

165

Detroit

but—they looked like they had walked out of the silver screen. His mother and Aunt Dorothy nearly swooned. Dad and Al were so handsome, their clothes impeccable, and their manners, "oh so European."

The impression the Pruchno brothers made on Michael has lasted over fifty years. Michael said the following about Dad, "Never have I disagreed with a man so fervently, yet loved him so intensely."

I asked Dad why they hadn't settled in Cleveland, where they had family. Dad told me they thought they'd have an easier time finding jobs in Detroit. Besides, they weren't going to meet their relatives looking for a handout.

After working at Huber Tool and Die for two years, Dad drove to the shop one morning and saw a police car sitting in the parking lot with its lights flashing. Dad's first thought was that there was a fire, and his personal measuring instruments were ruined. Soon Dad learned that the local union had organized a strike because a worker had been fired. Dad went to the union hall, with the other workers, and heard the speeches about how they shouldn't go back to work without a signed contract. Dad didn't really understand why he needed the union to protect his job; he reasoned that good work was protection enough.

Soon Dad got a call from the owner of Huber who asked Dad if he had been treated well. Dad answered that he had. He then asked if Dad had received any raises, and again Dad answered that he had. So the owner asked Dad to come back to work. He explained that the union was legally obligated to let the workers pass the picket line, and the sheriff was there to protect them. Dad agreed, and went back to work the next day, but the atmosphere was uncomfortable. There were very few people working, and Dad worried all day that his car might be vandalized. He resolved not to return to work until the contract had been settled.

Dad was friendly with a fellow worker from Huber, a very nice guy, who was quite a bit older than him. He told Dad that it may take months for them to settle, and that he couldn't afford to wait; he had a mortgage to pay. He suggested that if Dad wanted, they could go job-hunting together. Dad thought it was a good idea; perhaps he could pick up some pointers on how to better portray himself on a job application. But Dad was flabbergasted at how much the man built himself up—he actually lied. Afterward Dad confronted him, and the man responded that Dad shouldn't worry so much. They wouldn't get complex jobs to do right away, and by the time their new bosses figured it out they would be back at their old jobs.

After a while the contract was settled, and the owner purchased a large boring mill. The new mill could machine twenty thousand pounds of cast iron die shoes at a time, and the owner wanted to run it twenty-four hours a day. The chief steward worked the day shift, and knowing Dad liked his overtime, he offered Dad a great opportunity—to work the night shift. Dad knew it wouldn't last forever, but in the meantime, he could make some good money, seven hundred dollars a week.

During Dad's twelve-hour shift, he was the only one working. The owner's brother-in-law sat in the glass walled foreman's office reading the newspaper and drinking coffee. Dad was not allowed to be there by himself—union rules.

The work Dad did created a lot of dust. When he went to the bathroom he could see in the mirror that his face was black and his eyes were red; he looked as though he had been working in a coal mine. Dad's landlady wanted to know why his pillows were so black; she thought he was using some sort of hair concoction.

Although the pay was great, the schedule was grueling. It was the spring of 1955, and all Dad did was work, sleep and eat. And he didn't sleep very well either, in the bright and hot room. He didn't even have time to watch TV. When the chief steward told him he was so busy with union business that he needed Dad to return to working the day shift, Dad was pleased. Not only had he made a lot of money, but he could finally return to a more normal lifestyle.

During the weekdays, Dad worked a ten-hour day, and on Saturday he worked only five to eight hours. So on Saturday nights he went out with Jewish girls, and on Sundays he slept in. Dad often went out again on Sunday nights. Once in while he didn't get home until very late, reminiscent of his days in Munich, and he would sit on the porch until he heard stirrings inside the house; then he would go in, change his clothes, and go to work.

Dad and Al moved in with another very nice older couple, that Gruna recommended. The place was great; the room was bigger and there was more closet space. One night Dad and Al went out for dinner and then to a B'nai B'rith party at the Albert Einstein Lodge; they came home late. Dad turned off the light and relaxed in bed while smoking a cigarette. The next thing he knew it was an hour later, and he felt a sharp pain in his back, like lice crawling on him. He turned over, but couldn't fall back to sleep, the pain was getting worse. Finally Dad jumped from the bed, turned on the light, and found the room filled with smoke. He woke Al and they saw a red glowing spot. The mattress was on fire!

Together they extinguished the fire by beating it with a towel. With difficulty Dad opened the window that had been painted shut, and the winter air quickly dissipated the smoke. The next day Dad called Abrasha; he needed help repairing the mattress before the landlady changed the sheets. Dad didn't want to make trouble for the Pesis. And that was the last time he ever smoked in bed.

Dad realized his brother was serious about a girl when he started coming home late at night. Her name was Gladys Ehrenreich.

Fall 1951 — Late 1960s

She was beautiful and smart (she had a degree in economics), and Al was in love.

They got married in Florida on August 30, 1953. Dad had met Gladys before, but she was quiet and rather shy, and it wasn't until they were in Florida that Dad got to know his sister-in-law a little better. Gladys' father and stepmother owned a small hotel, the Alden, in Miami Beach, which they operated only in the winter since it wasn't air-conditioned, so there was plenty of room to host a summer wedding and the guests.

Dad flew down for the occasion; it was his first time in an airplane. The plane was practically empty, only three passengers including Dad. They were served an excellent steak dinner and were shown the pilot's cabin where they could marvel at the controls—no heightened security back then.

George Zak and his family flew down as well. Dad rented a red Chevy convertible, and Michael recalled Dad taking them for a ride, going wonderfully fast, with him and his brothers sitting on the folded-up top and their legs dangling into the back seat. According to Michael, Dad was the life of the party.

The wedding itself was a simple affair, and afterward Al and Gladys moved into a fancy hotel. Meanwhile, Dad sat in the Alden bar until the wee hours of the morning, waiting for his room to cool down.

The next day Dad was driving along when he saw his brother and sister-in-law crossing the street. He was on his way to see about renting a boat and going fishing. So he asked if they wanted to join him—it would be his treat. Dad had always liked the water and boats, and even better, they would be on the open ocean.

The group, consisting of Dad and four couples, went out on a five-hour fishing excursion. Dad caught a large fish, but had no idea how to reel it in. The captain told Dad it was too big to bring in anyway, so he let it go. This accomplishment under his

Detroit

belt, Dad went to the upper deck and relaxed in the sun until they came to shore.

When they returned to Detroit, the newlyweds moved into an apartment for the first six months of their marriage, before buying a house on Annchester, off Eight Mile Road. A little over a year later they started their family. They had three children—Rachel, Charles, and William.

It felt strange to Dad, not living with Al, they had been together for so long. But Dad was confident he would get married someday too, something to look forward to. Dad looked good with his Florida tan, and people were trying to fix him up—after all, it was his turn.

As a wedding present, Dad gave the couple a generous gift of five hundred dollars; he figured they could use the money. Dad also let Al have the Chevy they shared. But he needed a car too, so together they bought Dad a Studebaker convertible. It was fun to drive around in a convertible again, especially on a date, but the soft top didn't operate well and was more trouble than it was worth.

Dad took out a few girls; he can't remember their names, he didn't go out with them for very long. Dad took one girl to a movie, and when they arrived she wouldn't get out of the car. Finally it dawned on Dad that she was waiting for him to open her door. Then there was the girl who was so short, that even in high heels she was too short. Another girl had an attractive face and pleasant personality, but she must have weighed over two hundred pounds. After that, Dad was "very busy" and kept to himself for a while.

Dad had met a girl named Sima Zonder at the home of acquaintances Shoshana and Yitzchak Bank. (Yitzchak had worked with Yechiel at the newspaper in Munich.) Sima was the first girl Dad had met when he came to the States. She was from Poland and

Fall 1951 — Late 1960s

had been in hiding during the war. She lived in Windsor, Canada, and came across the river to visit her uncle in Detroit on the weekends. They had met on a Friday and she called Dad two days later. Dad thought, if she had the guts to call him, he wouldn't insult her by brushing her off. So they went out.

For a while they saw each other frequently on the weekends, but then it turned into an on-again/off-again relationship that finally ended when Dad met Mom. Although she moved to Israel, they remained friends. They still call each other on Rosh Hashanah to extend wishes for a happy, healthy New Year.

Eventually Dad recovered from his traumatic series of blind dates and was ready to try again. One of Gladys' aunts told him there was a girl he should meet, but first he had to get the consent of Mrs. Feigenson. Dad thought—what could he lose—after all he would be meeting the owner of Faygo Beverages, a soda company famous for its Redpop and Rock & Rye. Dad called Mrs. Feigenson, they spoke in Yiddish on the phone, and Dad felt heymish with her, meaning they had a good down-to-earth rapport.

One evening Dad went to her house, nicely dressed of course. Mrs. Feigenson was a petite woman who took him by the arm and led him to the library where she did all the talking. Dad waited until she sat down before he did, and his good manners were not lost on her. She explained that she had known the girl's mother for a long time; they belonged to the same Jewish organization. The son had a doctorate in chemistry and the daughter was a schoolteacher. About half an hour later Dad said, "Now you've seen me, do you have a picture of the girl, I should see her?" Mrs. Feigenson replied, "You will see her in person, pictures don't mean a lot, you need to talk to a person." She then gave Dad her name and number—Muriel Bello—who was to become my Mom.

Detroit

Dad couldn't imagine Mrs. Feigenson fixing him up with an "elephant" after meeting him, so he called Muriel. It was a short conversation; they made a date for a Saturday evening, shortly after Pesach in the spring of 1956. Muriel still lived with her parents, Rose (Galanter) and Max Bello, not far from Dad. They lived in an apartment near Dexter, in the old Jewish neighborhood where they owned a grocery store. Muriel made a good first impression on Dad; she was attractive, very nicely dressed and beautifully groomed, with gorgeous red nails. She was also on the zaftig (buxom) side, just the way Dad liked his women, with something to grab onto. (I can't recall how many times Dad has told me that I'm too skinny, his latest comment being, "Trust me, I know from too skinny.")

They went to a movie and out for a bite to eat. There was a deli at Seven Mile and Wyoming, Boesky, a very popular place, and on a Saturday night the wait was half an hour or longer. Muriel knew the manager, a friend of her best friend's brother. When he saw her, the maitre d' came right over, apologized for having kept them waiting, and immediately showed them to a table. I remember Mom telling me she didn't know what to order, she didn't want to offend her date, so she let him order first. When he ordered corned beef (not a kosher variety), she felt free to do the same. Mom introduced Dad to the "Dinty Moore" sandwich; his favorite for a long time—hot corned beef, Swiss cheese, coleslaw, and Russian dressing on rye.

Dad asked Muriel how she liked his broken English. (In his head, he was still translating from the German.) She told him she was used to it, that her parents still hadn't mastered the language. They were originally from Russia and had come to the States shortly after WWI. Dad asked if she knew Yiddish. She had gone to Yiddish school after public school, like kids today go to Hebrew school. She could understand everything perfectly, but she spoke a "broken" Yiddish. It didn't matter; Dad enjoyed listening to her anyway. She told him that she really liked to drive, and with a loan from her uncle had just bought herself a new car; she was very excited about it.

When Dad brought her home, he invited her for a boat ride the next day on Walled Lake. She replied that she didn't know how to swim. Dad promised that if the boat tipped over he'd save her. Muriel had a great time, and Dad enjoyed watching her every move. The following week Dad took her to see the play *South Pacific* and then out for dinner. That was the night he kissed her for the first time.

When Dad met Muriel, he was considering changing jobs. One Sunday he saw an ad in the newspaper for a position at Johansen Gauge Co. They needed skilled workers willing to work long hours, including weekends, at their facility in Dearborn. Johansen's headquarters and the main plant were located in Sweden. Old man Johansen used to work with Henry Ford making special precision instruments. To make a long story short, Dad got a new job.

Dad told them he could start in a week; he wanted to give notice where he worked, and they liked his conscientiousness. A week after starting at Johansen, Dad befriended a guy who told him he had made a big mistake in quitting his old job. For the past five years Johansen hadn't given anyone seniority; they would let workers go after eighty-nine days, just one day shy. Immediately Dad called his former employer and asked for his old job back. He was told, "Just bring your tools."

When Dad told his new superintendent he was quitting, the man wanted to know why. Dad explained without informing on his friend. The superintendent looked Dad in the eye and said he would grant Dad instant seniority if he would stay. Dad was bewildered, he had never heard of such a thing happening before. The superintendent called over the chief steward and they arranged it.

173

Detroit

Dad stayed at Johansen Gauge for fourteen years, until new management mismanaged it. During that period Dad got laid off a few times, since he was the last one hired, but he always got his job back. They liked him; they gave him overtime and he was their highest paid worker. Dad enjoyed working there and thought that was where he would retire.

Once Dad started at Johansen and felt more financially secure, he started thinking seriously about marrying Muriel. She always seemed to have the right answers. In regards to keeping a kosher home, she could go either way; one set of dishes or two, whatever Dad wanted—but she would never bring trayf (not kosher food) into her home.

Dad always saw to it that they had a good time. Every Saturday night they went out and Sundays too, occasionally Dad even called during the week. They went to the theatre or the movies and out for dinner. Sometimes Mom ate twice, first with her parents, and then with Dad.

But it was Dad who was the big eater. As he said, "I didn't eat like a pig, I ate like two pigs." Dad just couldn't gain a pound. Once he even went to a doctor to see if something was wrong with him. The doctor told him to get out of his office—"Just wait until you get older." Mom told me that once when they went clothes shopping, the salesman asked her if Dad was a professional boxer.

They had a good summer together, and in the fall Muriel went back to work, teaching elementary school. After Rosh Hashanah, in October 1956, Dad decided to propose, but first he had to become an American citizen. He didn't want to give Muriel a reason to later claim that it was only a marriage of convenience.

Dad studied hard for his citizenship exam. He was a bit nervous; there were so many things he didn't know. But the only question the judge asked him was, "Did you have sex?" Dad was a thirty-year-old man, how was he supposed to answer that question? So with a straight face he said, "No, your honor."

Dad got his citizenship papers and made a reservation at a famous nightclub in Windsor, the Elmwood, a place Muriel had always wanted to go. They had a nice dinner; there was music and dancing. Dad had his little speech memorized, and before he could finish it, she said yes. Dad thanked her for not making him wait too long. The next day Dad went to her parents' home with another little speech, and they drank a l'chaim.

The following Sunday Dad was invited to the Bellos for dinner. When everyone was seated, Muriel's mother served the appetizer, chopped liver. After a few bites, Dad felt something sharp in his mouth. At first he thought he had broken a tooth, so he pushed it from side to side, not wanting to appear ill mannered by putting his fingers in his mouth or spitting it out. As everyone was eating, Dad was thinking—it wasn't his tooth, it was too big and too sharp—it must be a piece of bone. He took his handkerchief, covered his mouth, and removed it. It was a piece of glass. Dad showed it to his future mother-in-law, and she got up and went into the kitchen. The blender was broken. She came back and quickly removed the plates. Later, when Dad and Muriel were alone he joked, "She barely knows me, and already she's trying to kill me!"

Dad wanted to buy Muriel an engagement ring, but her mother was concerned that he might inadvertently buy an imitation. She must have thought—what does this greener know about diamonds? Besides Dad's experience in Munich, he was also friendly with a watchmaker who knew where to get a reliable stone, and he accompanied Dad as well. Dad bought Muriel a one-and-a-quarter karat diamond ring with two baguettes set in platinum, the standard setting at the time.

Muriel bought Dad a dozen monogrammed dress handkerchiefs. Dad thought that wasn't exactly a fair exchange, but he didn't say anything; in fact, he still has some of them. She also

Detroit

surprised Dad with a very attractive Danish modern bedroom set, which she paid for and had delivered before their big day.

Mom and Dad were married on February 12, 1957, during her school vacation. It was on a Tuesday, a day considered lucky for marriages in the Jewish tradition. According to Dad, the hardest part about getting married was being scrutinized by the relatives. He wasn't very good at small talk then.

The wedding was held at the Shaeffer Furniture Association in Detroit. Rabbi Levine of Congregation Beth Tikvah, formerly of Shavl, officiated. Al and a pregnant Gladys were there, as were Gruna and Abrasha, and a fair number of the Zaks. Mrs. Feigenson was also among the one hundred or so guests. Dad wore a tuxedo, and I still have the T-length dress Mom wore, in a box next to mine, although it has yellowed with age. There was dinner, music and dancing, and when the guests left there was a blanket of snow on the ground. Dad had a good time, but was happy enough to put it behind him and get on with his life.

They went to New York City for their honeymoon. It was Dad's first time back since his arrival in the States over six years before. Dad was surprised they survived the taxi ride from the airport to their hotel near Central Park. They stayed for one week and did all the things people do when they go to New York. They ate in fine restaurants and went to museums, the Empire State Building, Rockefeller Center and Radio City Music Hall. They saw the "Old Lady"—the Statue of Liberty, and of course they went to the theatre.

They saw the play *Ann Frank*. Nobody applauded; it was like going to a funeral. It was also the only time Dad mentioned the Holocaust to his wife, other than to say he would never buy German products. He spoke very little of his family; basically Mom learned when he needed to light Yahrtzeit candles for his parents and sister.

Fall 1951 — Late 1960s

Ironically, while they were walking around town, Dad spotted the younger brother of one of his classmates from home. They went for coffee, and Mom got to hear all about who survived and what they were doing.

When they returned from their honeymoon they moved in with Mom's parents, in their new home at 22171 Cloverlawn in Oak Park. After three months, my grandparents decided to move to California, at least for the time being—their son Jacob was out there. The house they gave to their daughter and son-in-law as a wedding present.

Four years later I was born. I spent my first six years in that house and remember it well enough to draw up its floor plan. It was a ranch with a combination living/dining room, kitchen, bath, three bedrooms, and a finished basement; it cost $18,500. I remember sitting at the dining room table and drawing with Dad. I remember hiding behind Mom as she lay on the white couch while we watched *The Wizard of Oz,* terrified as the flying monkeys swooped down and captured Dorothy. I remember watching the Beatles on the *Ed Sullivan Show* after I had already been put to bed; the door had been left ajar and I could see the TV perfectly.

One day my parents brought my brother, Robert Charles, home from the hospital, an event of which I have no memory. When Bob was two-years-old, we moved to Southfield. Dad didn't want to move, he felt the Oak Park house was big enough, and more importantly, it was paid for. But Mom felt we would have to move eventually; she wanted her children in a better school system. Although upset, Dad relented. We moved to a street called Glenmorra, just around the block from Al, who had moved into the subdivision a few years before on Potomac Street. Dad figured; if he was moving, he might as well be close to his brother again.

Detroit

Al, Gruna Pesis and Dad
the brothers with Abrasha's wife, in Detroit, looking European.

Gladys Ehrenreich & Al Pruchno
engaged to be married.

Fall 1951 — Late 1960s

Muriel Bello & Sam Pruchno—Mom & Dad
while dating.

Max & Rose Bello
Mom's parents in front of their grocery store.

Detroit

Mom & Dad
on their wedding day—1957.

Fall 1951 — Late 1960s

The Cleveland Zaks at Mom and Dad's wedding
*beginning with woman in foreground and moving counterclockwise—
Henrietta & Dave; Dorothy & Max and Anna;
Michael and George & Terry and Kenny.*

Dad, Marcia and Bob
on their front lawn in Oak Park—1966.

NORTHVILLE

✫ ✫ ✫

LATE 1960S — SUMMER 1985

In the late 1960s, as Johansen Gauge was floundering, Dad, one of the last employees, prepared to go out on his own. He was only working forty hours a week, so he had plenty of time. Even so, he took time off work to attend an auction to purchase his first piece of equipment, a milling machine. The other bidders thought he was crazy for bidding so high, but he had examined it closely beforehand and saw that it came with a box of tools worth as much as the machine itself. Dad and a man named John split the cost of the equipment and rented space from a one-man shop on Telegraph Road. They started to build dies for Washer Inc., a large company where John had connections. They were making good money, twenty-five dollars an hour, and Dad wanted to build up the business. John, however, wasn't interested in anything more than making a few extra dollars. When Dad realized they didn't share the same objective, he bought John out.

Dad had no credit line for his emergent business, so every week he'd ask Mom for cash, $500 here, $300 there. Smiling, she asked him, "Don't you ever bring in money anymore?" Dad assured her, "It's coming, it's coming."

On a hot summer day in the early 1970s, Dad was driving around looking for work. When he realized how far he had driven, he exited the expressway at Novi Road. Near the fire department, he saw a garage with its door open, tool and die machinery inside, and some men working. Business was slow everywhere, yet these men were working—on a Saturday.

Dad walked in and introduced himself to the owner, Tony Kushigian. His company was called Normac, Inc. As Tony continuously smoked, Dad explained that he had a small machine shop and could do work for him at the same rate he was paying his own men. Dad didn't have any business cards so he wrote his contact information on a piece of paper. For some reason Tony kept that paper for over a year, and on Erev Yom Kippur, just as Dad was dressing for shul, he called.

They met the following Sunday and Tony gave Dad a little work to do. When he brought in the completed job, Dad asked when he could expect to be paid, mentioning he'd been stiffed before. Tony didn't even inspect Dad's work before telling his secretary to write a check for five thousand dollars. Dad left with check in hand, convinced it was going to bounce—but it cleared. Tony continued to have work for Dad, and about six months later he asked Dad to go into business with him.

Dad didn't have the necessary capital—$200,000—to become a fifty-fifty partner. What money he had was tied up in a real estate investment in Chicago with his friend from Munich, Joe Dembo. So he asked his brother if he would be his silent partner. One Sunday Dad took Al to see the shop. As Dad observed, "It didn't appeal to him." It just wasn't very impressive compared to Al's place of employment, Ford Motor Co.

Dad worked at Normac for about a year when Tony decided the time was right to relocate the business to Hendersonville, North Carolina. The new shop he had built on East Baseline Road, near the Northville Cider Mill, was already too small. Tony had always wanted to live in North Carolina, with its mountains and mild winters, and he wanted Dad to move with him.

That summer Dad took us on a family vacation down south, to check it out. "Jesus Saves" billboards were everywhere, and there was no evidence of Yiddishkeit (Jewishness). I hated it, and

Late 1960s — Summer 1985

I threatened to move in with Unc should Mom and Dad actually decide to move there. Mom gave me something to think about when she said, "How do you know your uncle would want you?" Thank God, they didn't like it either.

Tony tried to persuade Dad, pointing out there was a Jewish community only forty-five minutes away in Asheville. But Dad's answer remained an unwavering no. Still, he had put so much of himself into the company that he decided he would stay on until they dismantled the shop, to ensure a smooth transition. Only then would he look for a new job.

Tony thought he could do all the work in North Carolina, but Dad proved to him on paper that he wouldn't remain price competitive. Even with the cost of shipping, it was cheaper to manufacture in Northville and assemble in Hendersonville, and the quality of the manufacturing was better in Northville. So Tony decided to keep the Michigan shop open, and the responsibility of running the place he entrusted to Dad.

The night Dad received the "news" he couldn't sleep; he thought Tony was crazy. The man barely knew him, how could he put him in charge? The next morning Dad couldn't wait to talk to him, "I could steal from you and you'd never know it until it was too late." Tony's response, "Go ahead—steal—so long as you show me a profit."

When Dad began at Normac, he had bought one hundred shares of company stock at thirty-five dollars per share. As a shareholder, he would fly down to North Carolina to attend the Board of Directors meetings. On one of these occasions Tony asked Dad to bring his wife along. Mom had graciously entertained Tony and his wife Norma when they had come to Michigan, and they wanted to reciprocate. But that was somewhat of a ruse. They actually wanted to formally appoint Dad Vice President of the company, just three years after he had started.

Dad never became a partner, but he did become the second largest stockholder. The old adage applies—behind every great man there is a great woman. It was because Mom worked, and they could virtually live off her salary, that Dad could keep putting his hard earned dollars back into the company. At one point Dad showed his brother the bonus check Tony had given him. Al realized his mistake; it was more than his salary. From almost nothing Tony and Dad built a nice million-dollar company that employed seventy people. Dad had achieved the American dream.

I knew Dad had become financially successful when in the late 1970s, with my college bills looming on the horizon, we went on not one, but two family vacations. Previously vacations were every other year, and they involved a lot of driving.

The first trip was to New York over Thanksgiving weekend. Like Mom and Dad on their honeymoon, we did all the things people do when they go to New York. We ate in fine restaurants, went to museums, and saw the city's great architecture, including the Old Lady. We went to the theatre to see *Beatlemania* for Bob and John Curry's *Icedancing* for me. For Dad, we stopped in what seemed like every camera store in the city.

That summer we went to California. We drove along the coast from Monterey to Carmel and went to Catalina Island. We saw the San Diego Zoo, and *Evita*, pre-Broadway. We toured Hearst Castle, and even though I hate the water, the pool was so enticing I begged Dad to "accidentally" push me in. Dad was tempted and still says, "I should've pushed you." Mom and Dad were finally enjoying the fruits of their labors.

Just four short years later, Mom became an insulin dependent diabetic. The following year she was diagnosed with ovarian cancer. After her first surgery, she had two rounds of monthly chemotherapy, which lasted about a year. Her veins were so thin and deep that the procedure became quite painful. Only one nurse could get the needle in the vein the first time, and Dad always tried to arrange for Mom to be her patient. He even offered to pay her to come in when it wasn't her shift.

When the chemo was complete, Mom wanted to go to Europe, a life long dream. Her doctor said it was O.K., as long as she didn't run and jump. There was no use going just to sit in a hotel, so Dad talked her into a Caribbean cruise instead. They would do Europe another time.

When they returned she had her second surgery. Basically the doctor just opened her up, looked around, and closed her; the cancer had spread considerably. So they found a new oncologist, a Lithuanian they heard performed miracles, and Mom began radiation treatments immediately.

Dad tried to prepare me for the inevitable, but I wouldn't listen. I could not conceive of the possibility that my Mom might die. But deep down I must have known it would happen; I had stopped eating and began incessantly reorganizing my bedroom. Dad had stopped sleeping and started grieving. Dad had truly expected to leave this world first; he was four years older and he used to smoke (not to mention the effect years of deprivation might have had on him). Mom lasted only two weeks under the doctor's care.

The day she died Dad had planned to spend at the hospital catching up on office paperwork. But a nurse called in the morning and told him to come right away—Mom's pulse was dropping. Dad was with her when she took her last breath, offering words of encouragement as she fought valiantly on, not ready to say goodbye to this life.

Figuring we had all day, Bob and I stopped to pick up Mom's first cousin, one of her best friends, Sandra Nerenberg. We had lunch at Taco Bell, and then we went to the hospital to visit with her. We were too late.

As I stared at Mom, her eyelid flickered, and my heart skipped a beat. I started crying that there must have been a mistake—

she's not dead! I did not know then that the nervous system could still send out signals.

She died on Sunday, August 31, 1985, just a few years after her father had passed away, but unfortunately before her mother.

When pressed for more information about Mom's illness and death, Dad only talked about Mom's overriding concern for her mother. Mom wanted to spare her anguish and had kept her illness a secret. Before Mom's chemo, she would visit her mother and make sure she had all the groceries she would need for the week. Mom knew she would not even be able to talk to her on the telephone for a few days after the procedure. Dad made her excuses; she was in the shower, she was shopping, or she was napping. When the chemo made her hair fall out, Mom even chose a wig with the same proportion of brown to silver as her natural hair—so grandma wouldn't suspect. And when her mother had recovered from yet another heart attack, Mom moved her from the hospital to a nursing home. She just had to make sure her mother would be taken care of, in the event that her own health deteriorated. Even though grandma was terribly upset and didn't understand why she couldn't go back to her apartment, Mom didn't say a word. In the end it was Dad who had the heart-rending task of telling his mother-in-law that her daughter had been sick with cancer—and that she had died.

Late 1960s — Summer 1985

The family at Bob's Bar Mitzvah
*front row—Dad and Al's children—Charlie, Marcia, Bob, Rachel and Billy
back row—Max & Rose Bello (Dad's in-laws), Dad & Mom, Al, and
Mamie & Ellis Pruchnie (Welsh cousins)—1978.*

Mom & Dad
at their surprise 25th wedding anniversary celebration—1982.

Northville

Al, Max Zak and Dad
the brothers with their first cousin at his 50th wedding anniversary celebration in Cleveland—1985.

Dad and Tony Kushigian
Vice President and President of Normac, Inc.

DACHAU — VISITED

✽ ✽ ✽

FALL 1985

Shortly after my Mom died, I met three of my architecture school friends in Europe for a "put-off-the-real-world" tour. I was never thrilled that Germany was part of the itinerary, but I figured if I had to be there, I would go to Dachau and take my goyish friends with me.

We went through the museum first, and fortunately for my traveling companions most of the verbiage was in German, or I would have read every word. I saw some photos I've seen reproduced many times over. But I found myself most intent on those pictures of men at hard physical labor; those I scanned for a glimpse of Dad.

Basically the museum left me cold, but walking around the grounds was another story. There was row after row of rectangles in the earth, foundations of the demolished barracks. One of the barracks had been reconstructed, and I imagined Dad walking around there. The crematoria still remained, and as I looked at the ovens I felt my anger rise. For the first time in my life I felt something for a grandmother and an aunt I never knew.

I said Kaddish for them at the Grave of Thousands, and again at the Memorial for the Six Million. I thought a lot about how much Dad had to endure in his life, and how much I respected and admired him. I left Dachau a bit disappointed; I was expecting a more transformative experience. But as Dad has said many

Fall 1985

times, "A person cannot possibly grasp what happened there, without going through it himself."

A day or two before I left on my grand adventure, Dad suggested that if I had the time to try and find the house he stayed in after the war, in Icking, just a half-hour drive outside of Munich. It was still owned by the Kalteneggers, although their name had escaped him at the time. He drew a very basic map showing the Isar River, the Rathaus (City Hall), the grocer, and a street with three houses on it, his being the last. He also gave me two photographs.

One was a picture of him standing in front of a nice house. He was wearing a long coat, holding his cap and gloves, and he had one foot up on a bench showing off those Russian style boots. Dad gave me that photo because it showed the house well, and he thought I'd be able to locate the street based on that house.

The second photo was also of him, standing in front of the house he stayed in. But it didn't show much of the house, just four feet or so of wall with some latticework, a portion of a window, and the beginning of the roofline. The front yard fence and the right entry gatepost were also visible. With the "map" and two photographs in hand, I thought there was no way we were ever going to find the place.

Like detectives searching for clues, we noticed that in the second photograph, the entry gatepost had a chip out of the right side of its cap piece. Incredibly, forty years later, we found a gatepost that matched; it hadn't been repaired or replaced. Everything else about the photograph had changed; the fence was different, the latticework was gone, but that chip remained! The street had changed too; with many more than three houses, it had taken on a more suburban character.

Dachau — Visited

As we stood there and stared at the house, then at the photo, and back again, the woman of the house saw us through her window, got nervous, and closed the curtains. So I went up to the front door and rang the bell. The entire family came to the door. I showed them the house in the photograph and asked if it could be their house. I explained that my Dad had lived there after the war.

They were very excited. They invited us in and gave us the grand tour. I saw the room Dad stayed in and we took pictures. They explained that the house had been in the family for generations, and Mr. Kaltenegger told us with pride that his grandfather had been in the SS. I was stunned. Dad had never explained the circumstances of how he had come to live in this house. I naively assumed that the people who had lived there at the time were Jewish sympathizers. But then I figured, if Dad could live there, I could be there for a few minutes. Dad later told me that he had seen pictures of the old man in uniform—he was Wehrmacht, not SS, although most likely a Nazi party member. Dad assured me that had the old man been in the SS, he would have had a "good time" with him. Dad suggested that they wanted to impress us with their grandfather's "pedigree"; or perhaps I just misunderstood them, English not being their first language.

Then they took us down the street, Kirchenstrasse, to find the house in the other photo. They didn't understand that the house held no interest for me, it was merely a reference point, but I think we located it just the same. After so many years the property was quite overgrown and the house was barely visible. As we continued our walk, we seemed to be the big news in town that evening, second only to the power outage caused by someone who crashed into an electrical pole. We passed a shop and Mr. Kaltenegger showed the pictures to a man named Wilhelm Buchmann, and he actually remembered Dad!

We returned to the Kaltenegger's and sat in the semi-darkness, as they served us a little bread, cheese, sausage and beer.

Mr. Kaltenegger further explained that his grandfather was forced to house Eastern European refugees after the war. Later Dad said that the old man couldn't even bring himself to talk with Dad, but his wife had graciously allowed Dad to host a wedding party for twenty-five in her home, using her china and good tablecloths. Dad teased me in his speech at my wedding about how he had put together a wedding celebration with just a few days notice, two dollars in his pocket, and without the help of a wedding planner.

In any event, Kaltenegger's descendants were very nice to us. They even gave me some photographs to take back to Dad. One was of a beautifully painted family tree that Dad remembered their grandfather working on.

What an amazing day that was—Dachau and Icking! It was as close as I'm ever going to get to my roots. Shavl, as Dad knew it, no longer exists.

Dachau — Visited

Dad
in front of the easily identifiable house, notice the boots.

Dad
in front of the house he stayed in, notice the chip in the gatepost.

These are the photographs Dad gave me with the hope that I would get to Icking.

Fall 1985

Marcia and Mrs. Kaltenegger
the author and the lady of the house—1985.

SOUTHFIELD

✮ ✮ ✮

FALL 1985 — SPRING 1991

A couple of months after Mom's death, Al's daughter Rachel got married in Philadelphia, and Dad became reacquainted with their next-door neighbor, Judith Mantel Schwartz. She too, had been recently widowed. Her husband Eugene, also a Survivor, had died after a protracted battle with cancer. They had two children. Debbie, a young bride, who had married just weeks before her father's death; and Daniel, a teenager, who was studying at a Yeshiva in Chicago.

As Dad and Judy conversed at Rachel's wedding, Judy offered Dad a home cooked meal, and Dad offered to fix whatever in her house needed fixing. At that moment their relationship began, and in sixteen months they were married.

Dad felt strongly that even his grown children needed a mother, and Judy did all those things a mother does. She made my brother and me feel at home, and she lent us her ear when we had a problem. She came in from out-of-town and helped when my son was born and embraced the role of grandma. More importantly, with Judy, Dad found someone to share the middle and later years of his life, which included an active social life and quite a bit of travelling.

Judy had originally come from Sibiu, Romania, and she had her own wartime stories of hardship and suffering. During the war, her father, Lazer, had been imprisoned, beaten and sent to a work camp. A neighbor offered to "adopt" Judy and her siblings

Southfield

if the situation got desperate, but these same neighbors donated their biscuit factory to be converted to a crematorium the moment the Nazis arrived. Risking his life, Judy's father escaped from the work camp just long enough to arrange for his wife Regina and their children to relocate. It was a dramatic change from their well-to-do residence to a shack located between a cemetery and German headquarters. But living so close to the Nazis, he thought, no one would suspect they were Jews.

Judy was eleven-years-old when they were liberated by the Soviets in August 1944, just one month before the crematorium was to become operational. After the war, life remained oppressive under the Communists. Judy, her parents and brothers, Heinrich (Bruder) and Joseph (Jojo), were not even permitted to leave Romania until 1962, fifteen years after their father had applied for an exit visa. When finally they were allowed to emigrate, they could not take anything with them; the police even confiscated the fur collar on Judy's coat. Then they had to spend a mandatory year in Paris before they were cleared to enter the United States. Judy's sister Eva, her husband Nathan Mendelsohn and their baby girl followed a year later.

Dad's brother Al died soon after his sixty-eighth birthday on June 12, 1991. He had survived his wife Gladys by over fifteen years and was survived by Arlene Fleisher Ellenson, his second wife.

Al had been in good shape; he would meet Dad at the health club a couple of times a week. And besides sitting in the shvitz, Al walked on the treadmill and rode the bicycle, good training for his upcoming month-long trek in the Himalayas. But Al knew something was wrong. In time he went to a doctor and was told he had prostate cancer. The doctor said he could go on his grand adventure, which was still a few months out, but that Al must come see him the moment he returned. Al felt fine after his travels, and he didn't go back to the doctor so quickly. He told Dad, "Nothing is wrong with me, the doctors just want my money." By the time he finally went, it was too late.

When Unc was literally on his deathbed he told me he owed his success in life to his brother, my Dad.

There had never been a time in Dad's life that he had been without Al. Even when they left Germany they had decided where to settle together. Dad missed his brother, his best friend. He missed having him to talk to and to argue with; he missed Al borrowing his tools and never returning them. Dad was truly alone in a way he had never been before; no one was alive who shared his memories of the past. Dad has never shaved off the moustache he grew while sitting Shiva for Al, almost twenty years ago.

Southfield

Judy (Mantel Schwartz) & Dad
enjoying married life again.

Dad, Judy, Marcia, Eli, Bob and Max
on an Alaskan cruise—2005.

DACHAU — REVISITED

✫ ✫ ✫

FALL 1997

Dad had been back to Germany on business a few times for the trade shows in Hanover, but he had never been back to Munich. He casually mentioned he was considering it, at which point I said, "Not without us, you aren't."

So forty-six years after he left Germany, Dad returned to Munich in September 1997 with his immediate family—Judy, Bob, Eli and me. Dad was a bit disappointed that Munich looked so good, that it showed no scars from the war. At the same time he seemed to take a kind of pride in the city, like people do when they know a foreign place very well, or when they are showing foreigners around their own town. Dad was excited to show us the glockenspiel, whose life sized figures performed at various times during the day. It was built into the neo-gothic city hall in the Marienplatz (the city center), Dad's old stomping grounds.

But this wasn't just a pleasure trip, and as it turned out we all had our roles to play. Eli was chief chauffeur and I was the navigator, while Bob filled in where needed. And although Dad and Judy could read the German signs, without us they would have been lost. Very little of what Dad had come to see was actually at the main camp of Dachau, since he was mostly at the satellite camps, nevertheless, that is where we started.

While at Dachau Dad was pretty testy—he wandered about and wandered off. I couldn't imagine what he was thinking. I wanted so much to say and do the right thing, and I'm sure everyone else did too, but everything everyone said and did seemed to come out wrong. As if it wasn't bad enough at that moment, we have the video to remind us of how awkward it was. Dad didn't want to speak or answer questions. He just wanted to say Kaddish, but forgot his kippah (skull cap), so Judy made one for him out of a handkerchief. Once we left Dachau, it was like Dad had come out of a trance, and we could all breathe a sigh of relief.

The next day we needed a vacation and played tourist. We went to Berchtesgaden, the Eagle's Nest, Hitler's hideout on top of a mountain. No wonder the man thought he could control the world—it's just you and God up there. We also went for a boat ride on Lake Konigsee, and Dad reminisced about the time he went skinny-dipping in that very lake. That evening we dined across the border in Salzburg, Austria.

The following day we returned to the business of retracing Dad's footsteps and went to Icking. We lunched al fresco, on a beautiful day, in a magnificent setting. It was fun, and Dad was the life of the party. I was then able to guide us, not without some difficulty, to the Kaltenegger's. When they opened the door, they recognized me. I introduced Dad, and they welcomed him and showed us around. They had done significant work on the house since I had been there a dozen years before; the arrangement of rooms on the first floor was totally different. Once again Dad saw the original painting of their family tree dating back to 1430.

Dad walked upstairs to the room he had stayed in, which looked much the same as when he lived there, and he made some jokes about his women guests. Dad recalled old man Kaltenegger doing his calisthenics outside in the early morning, summer and winter, and calling out for his wife, "Clara, Clara!" The old man's grandson chuckled, as he too remembered a similar scene.

It was in the backyard that Dad really felt the passage of time. There he saw a fully mature tree he remembered as being nothing more than a sapling. He also remembered where the chickens and rabbits were kept in their cages, now long gone. In fact,

Dachau — Revisited

the photograph of Dad holding a sword in fighting stance, on the cover of this book, was taken in this very yard.

We took our leave of the Kalteneggers, but we weren't quite ready to move on. So we strolled around the neighborhood a bit while Dad remarked on this and that, a neighbor's BMW, his motorcycles—the important things.

We then continued our driving tour, and Dad pointed out the Sanatorium run by the SS doctor. Dad really wanted to find the house he had escaped to from the Death March, but that was like looking for a needle in a haystack.

We were, however, easily able to follow the path of the Death March. Two years prior, fourteen statues had been erected marking the route, for the commemoration of the fiftieth anniversary of the liberation of Dachau. We didn't see them all, but a good number of them. The statues were all the same, or variations, made of bronze, about two feet high by five feet long, and set on stone bases about five feet off the ground. The statues depicted featureless people draped in thin sheets so their bodies looked neither naked nor clothed; they were huddled together, walking.

Each statue bore a plaque with the following inscription—*HIER FUHRTE IN DEN LETZIEN KRIEGSTAGEN IM APRIL 1945 DER LEIDENSWEG DER HAFTLINGE AUS DEM KONZENTRATIONSLAGER DACHAU VORBEI INS UNGEWISSE.* Dad and Judy translated it as, "Here in the last war days in April 1945, the road of sorrow of the prisoners of the concentration camp Dachau, on the walk of the unsure, the way to the unknown."

Dad was most interested, however, in finding the locations of the satellite camps, which proved much more difficult than anticipated. Whenever we walked by someone Dad's age or older, i.e. someone who might actually know where these camps were located, Dad was always treated the same way—people couldn't get away from him fast enough. In their haste they uttered, "Why do you want to go there?" "That was a long time ago, it's over and done with." "Forget about it." As a result, the days of our trip were flying by with little accomplished.

Fall 1997

It wasn't until our last day in Germany that we met with some success. It was Shabbat, and Dad, Bob and I went to Landsberg. Judy and Eli couldn't come; Judy was Shomer Shabbos (observant of the laws of Shabbat) and Eli needed to go to shul to say Kaddish for his father.

We headed out, expecting to come back a few hours later having struck out yet again. But this time Dad used a different tactic. He questioned the younger people; those who would be the sons and daughters of those he tried to speak to previously. They were much more agreeable and actually tried to be helpful. Then we met with success.

Dad spoke with a woman who knew the local historian; she even brought us over to his house and introduced us. He was a musician and had an engagement to attend, but he telephoned his son and explained to him where to take us. He came with his wife and baby, and they schlepped us around for the next five hours.

They took us to a number of satellite campsites, and astonishingly, there was hardly any evidence of what had actually happened there. The camps had been dismantled, with only the random hunk of concrete remaining. But occasionally, amidst the overgrown vegetation, you'd come across a large rough-hewn stone with an inscription in German memorializing a spot in the middle of nowhere, and wonder who was ever going to read, "By night to light—Here rest concentration camp victims."

They also took us to a place, which we could only see at a distance, since it was behind a fence with a sign that read "Military Security Area." It was the German Air Force Repair Facility, the one bunker that had been completed after the war, not the exact one Dad was enslaved at, but one of the three.

When we finally returned to the hotel, Judy was beside herself with worry, and Eli, confident nothing bad had happened to us, was just angry. We had neglected to stop and call the hotel to let them know what was going on. And yes, I still hear about it. But Dad is still in contact with these good people, Juwitha and Christoph Ziegler, who aided him in his quest.

Dachau — Revisited

Dad
at the Kaltenegger house in Icking—1997.

Fall 1997

Dad
back at Dachau—1997.
with the former service building, currently a museum, and commemorative sculpture, depicting the anguish of the prisoners.

Dad
at a gravestone in the middle of nowhere, notice the Jewish star at the upper right hand corner.

SOUTHFIELD — RETIREMENT

✭ ✭ ✭

SUMMER 2002 — PRESENT

Dad retired from Normac in the summer of 2002 at the age of seventy-five, with much pomp and ceremony. Eli and I drove in for the day to attend the party. But now I was concerned—what was Dad going to do with his time? He never had any hobbies. He only worked and then worked some more. But had he known retirement was going to be so fulfilling, he would have done it a long time ago.

Dad started doing those things I suppose he always wanted to do, but never had the time. He started studying with a rabbi every day, Rabbi Greenfield of Oak Park, continuing an education that ceased with the Soviet invasion. I tease Dad that one day he'll become too religious to eat in my home—it won't be kosher enough. Dad had been raised Shomer Shabbos, but he took a long intermission from Judaism. He still observed the major holidays, but from a cultural rather than religious perspective. However, as he got older he reasoned, if he wasn't a member of God's club on Judgment Day, he might not get the opportunity to have his questions answered, questions which have troubled him since the war.

Dad also returned to drawing and painting. Since helping his sister Maša with her school projects so long ago, and introducing me, his daughter Marcia, to drawing, his talents had laid dormant. He started out by taking a few simple art classes, learning how to work with charcoal, pastels, watercolors and oils. But with no time to waste, he hired a private instructor.

Southfield — Retirement

Dad does not suffer from a lack of self-confidence. He learned the basics quickly and then began his ambitious projects. For example, his first attempt at portraiture was a triple. He painted Eli, Max and me on a single canvas, and his rendering of his grandson was truly inspired.

Whenever I'd come to town, my first stop was always, and still is, his studio. He'd want my opinion, because as he says, "You're the only one who is honest with me." I'm not about to tell him something is good when it isn't; he's been lovingly critical of me all my life. Dad is not an expressionist, or impressionist, or abstractionist—he's a realist, and his style is painstaking.

The project dearest to him is his Holocaust Series. His motivation was the lack of images on the subject. He would find bits and pieces, but nothing that thoroughly captured the events that remained vivid in his memory. He completed four paintings, fairly large pieces, measuring well over three feet by four feet. Even his signature bears witness to the events, for it includes his Dachau number, 84782. His first painting was entitled *Roll Call*. Dad rendered over twelve hundred people in this incredibly detailed painting, which took him about a year to complete. It now hangs, on loan, in the Holocaust Memorial Center in Farmington Hills, Michigan, and it can also be viewed on their website.

The U.S. Holocaust Memorial Museum in Washington D.C. wanted it as well, as did Yad Vashem in Israel, but they only display Holocaust art painted during the war. Both museums would take care of it in perpetuity, loan it to other museums and galleries wanting to exhibit it, and show it on their website. However, I had an image of that final scene in *Raiders of the Lost Ark*, where it would sit in a box next to the Ark of the Covenant in a room the size of a football field—and be forgotten.

I'm very glad Dad decided to have *Roll Call* and the others—*Genocide by Labor*, *Death March* and *Liberation*, hung in his "hometown." It is there where people know him, where he lectures, where his video testimony can be seen, and where he can enjoy his accolades.

Currently Dad has shifted his focus to religious themes. His first, of what will hopefully be many paintings, is of the Kol Nidre prayer *Labrit Habet*. It includes seven separate vignettes as it compares clay in the hands of a potter, stone in the hands of a mason, and so on, to the Jewish people in the hands of God, and thus Dad's title *In God's Hands*. This too hangs on loan in the Holocaust Memorial Center. Anything Dad paints, they want. He really has become somewhat of a local celebrity.

Southfield — Retirement

Roll Call
Samuel Pruchno 84782
2005, oil on canvas, over 36" x 48"
on loan at the Holocaust Memorial Center, Farmington Hills, Michigan

This painting illustrates what Dad considered to be one of the cruelest experiences of the concentration camp, the counting of prisoners, which could take hours a day. There are approximately twelve hundred prisoners depicted here, including Dad and his brother Al, with their actual numbers shown on their uniforms, 84782 and 86018. In fact, all the numbers shown represent real people. Dad obtained them from the Dachau archives.

Summer 2002 — Present

Genocide by Labor
*Samuel Pruchno 84782
2008, oil on canvas, over 36" x 48"
on loan at the Holocaust Memorial Center, Farmington Hills, Michigan*

One of the most physically demanding jobs in the concentration camp was the unloading of cement bags from the trains. The prisoners provided the slave labor used to construct the Ringeltaube, the three semi-subterranean bombproof bunkers in the Landsberg area. From the air these airplane-manufacturing facilities would not be seen.

Southfield — Retirement

Death March
Samuel Pruchno 84782
2006, oil on canvas, over 36" x 48"
on loan at the Holocaust Memorial Center, Farmington Hills, Michigan

The prisoners were forced to walk through this bucolic setting, down the spiral road outside Wolfratshausen, away from the approaching American troops. Al is supporting Dad, in the lower left portion of the painting, as Dad comes to the end of his strength. A color enlargement of this section can be seen on the back cover, as well as the houses on the front.

Summer 2002 — Present

Liberation
Samuel Pruchno 84782
2007, oil on canvas, over 36" x 48"
on loan at the Holocaust Memorial Center, Farmington Hills, Michigan

Dad, in the lower center of the painting, looks more like a reporter than a prisoner after he escaped the Death March. From the tank, American soldiers are throwing Hershey bars down to those they liberated. The line of approaching vehicles represent the future transporting of displaced persons home—that is, everyone except the Jews. However, a grouping of Survivors and the cloud directly above them represents the future State of Israel, a place many would come to call home. Dad was impressed that his grandson Max recognized this imagery the moment he saw it.

Southfield — Retirement

Dad and Max
"working" on Genocide by Labor—*2007*.

THE CONVERSATION

✡ ✡ ✡

FALL 2006

In November, our extended family was in Iowa City for David's Bar Mitzvah (Al's grandson). We were only steps away from shul for Friday night dinner and services when Max asked Dad, "So Grandpa, tell me what it was like in a concentration camp?" Dad told him it was a long conversation and there wasn't enough time right then; they would have to talk about it later.

Max didn't miss a beat. The moment we walked out of shul to return to the hotel Max asked him again. Dad shot me a look that said—I don't believe this kid, he's only six, where is this coming from, and how shall I answer him? Dad explained that it was sort of like being in jail, and Max replied, "Don't you mean it was more like being a slave?" Dad had to agree.

Max then proceeded to question Dad about all the small day-to-day things that nobody thinks to talk or write about, but everyone would like to know about. Things like—What did you get to eat? What was the bathroom like? Where did you sleep? How often did you get to change your clothes? And on, and on…

I didn't hear all the questions Max asked, or the responses Dad gave, for they were walking a few paces ahead having a private conversation. However, after Max went to bed that night, Dad said to me, "Mashki, if you told me he had asked you those questions—I would not have believed you."

THE BLESSING

✧ ✧ ✧

WINTER 2010

During a recent winter in Miami Beach, Dad and Judy attended a lecture given by Rabbi Lazar Brody at their neighborhood synagogue, The Shul. At its conclusion, people went up to the prominent rabbi to ask for a blessing, a common practice in Breslover Hasidic communities. Dad asked for a blessing as well.

He explained to the rabbi that he was a Holocaust Survivor and was having trouble with his leg. Dad had broken his hip a couple of years ago and was still experiencing pain.

Since Survivors were only steps away from death simply because they were Jews, from a religious perspective, they have sanctified God's name. And so Rabbi Brody took Dad's hands in his and placed them on his own head saying, "No—you bless me."

May Dad bless us all.

THE DESCENDANTS

✯ ✯ ✯

FALL 1954—PRESENT

Dad and Al's story would be incomplete without listing their descendants. After all, Hitler did not win. Combined the Pruchno brothers have five children and eight grandchildren.

Samuel Pruchno and Muriel Bello's children:

    Marcia Lynn (Malka Leah bat Shmuel)

    Robert Charles (a.k.a. Bob) (Chaim Yitzchak Rachmiel ben Shmuel).

Samuel and Muriel's grandson:

    From Marcia Pruchno and Eli Lawrence:

        Max Reuben (Reuven Matan ben Eliyahu Yosef).

Albert Pruchno and Gladys Ehrenreich's children:

    Rachel Ann (Rachel Chaya bat Avraham)

    Charles Jonathan (a.k.a. Charlie) (Chaim Yitzchak ben Avraham)

    William Bernhard (a.k.a. Billy) (Zev ben Avraham).

Fall 1954—Present

Albert and Gladys' grandchildren:

From Rachel Pruchno and Jonathan Brill:

Elaine Alyssa (Aliza Elkah bat Yonatan Yitzchak)

Louis Arin (a.k.a. Ari) (Lozar Avraham ben Yonatan Yitzchak).

From Charlie Pruchno and Marcia Willing:

Gabrielle Lili (Zahava Leah bat Chaim Yitzchak)

Abraham David (a.k.a. David) (Avraham David ben Chaim Yitzchak).

From Billy Pruchno and Dana Goldhar:

Jacob Aaron (a.k.a. Jake) (Yacob Aron ben Zev)

Eli Micah (Eliyahu ben Zev)

Lilly Zahavah (Shoshana Zahavah bat Zev).

The Descendants

Dad, Marcia and Bob
at Daniel (Judy's son) and Tamara's wedding—1998.

Marcia & Eli and Max
the author and her family—2001.

Fall 1954—Present

Al's girls at his grandson Ari's Bar Mitzvah
Elaine (Rachel's daughter), Gabrielle (Charlie's daughter), Rachel (Al's daughter), Dana (Billy's wife), Marcia Willing (Charlie's wife) and little Lilly (Billy's daughter)—2009.

Al's boys at his grandson Ari's Bar Mitzvah
David (Charlie's son), Charlie (Al's son), little Eli (Billy's son), Jonathon (Rachel's husband), Billy (Al's son), Jake (Billy's son) and Ari (Rachel's son)—2009.

The Descendants

Dad and Max
l'dor v'dor—from generation to generation—2009.

EPILOGUE

I had help with the genealogy on both sides of Dad's family tree, which I include here for posterity's sake. I did not include it within the story because it is not part of Dad's memory. Besides, some of the information I present is contradictory or incomplete, and could use further investigation, but that is beyond the scope of this memoir.

On Dad's Father's side, information was provided by Michael Pruchnie, our Welsh cousin, who had visited Lithuania on his personal quest for our shared family tree. Michael was not content to let two middle-aged men, his father, Ellis, and my Uncle Al, who met on a flight from Israel in 1977, take one look at each other and declare—yes, we are related! Michael worked with a renowned expert in the derivation of Jewish names and the head archivist of the Lithuania State Archives in Vilna. He traced our common ancestor back to Shemariah Pruchno, born about 1820. Shemariah would be Dad, Al and Ellis's great-grandfather. Michael was even able to go back one more generation to Sheine Bat Leiba Pruchno born in 1799.

According to Michael, Dad's Father, Chaim Yitzchak Pruchno, was born on December 22, 1877, and his younger brother Boris was born on March 5, 1885. Michael also discovered that there had been three sisters, born between the brothers, but they all had died before their first birthdays. Although Dad didn't recall his Father ever mentioning them, it would explain the seven-year age difference between the men.

However, in 1987 Al had filled out paperwork regarding his parents and sister at Yad Vashem (the Holocaust museum in

Israel), which was contrary to Michael's later research. Al had written that his Father was born in 1895, his Mother in 1898, and Maša in 1921. Dad said that Maša was born in 1919, and from the family photograph (see chapter *Shavl—Childhood*) it is clear that Maša is more than two years older than Al. When it came to their birth years, Dad thought Al was just making an educated guess.

If Dad's Father was born in 1877, he would have been sixty-years-old when Dad was ten, but Dad does not remember his Father being "so old." However, a child's perception of an adult's age is dubious at best. My own ten-year-old's dad is fifty-five, and he is an only child, not the last of four, so perhaps the large age difference between Dad and his Father only seems a bit unusual for the time.

For the majority of his life, Dad thought his Father had come to this country in the 1920s, after his parents stay in Moscow. It wasn't until I did an Ellis Island name search that I learned he had arrived on August 30, 1905, on the ship *Caronia* out of Liverpool. The ship manifest noted that his ethnicity was Russian and Hebrew, his marital status was single, his age was twenty-six, and his last place of residence was Libau (then Russia, currently Latvia). It also listed his first name as Isidor, clearly a name he was known by since Dad suggested I use it in my search. As confirmation, I recently saw a letter he had written in Yiddish to his brother-in-law Ben in 1922, which he signed, in English, Isidor Pruchno. It was given to me by his granddaughter, my cousin Anna. And so I am reasonably certain this was Dad's Father, and it corroborates his birth date as provided by Michael, within a couple of years.

On Dad's Mother's side, I had help from an unexpected source. A stranger by the name of Gilda Kurzman contacted Dad while we were working on this project. She too scoured the Lithuanian birth, marriage, death, and census records, which she admitted were notorious for being inaccurate, for a project of her own. She was looking for descendents of Pusalotas and helped establish a website about the small town.

She provided me with information on two other siblings Dad had no knowledge of, a sister and a brother—Chana, born in 1867, and Meyer Leyb, born in 1871 (died 1888). She also had birth years for Dad's Mother's brother in Cleveland, Benjamin, 1875, and for her sister in Warsaw, Sonia, 1877.

However, Sonia's birth year is also questionable. Her nephew George Zak had entered her birth year into the Yad Vashem database as 1885. He had also listed birth years for the rest of her family—husband Morris, 1880, and sons Solomon and Gutek, 1912 and 1916.

Unfortunately Gilda had no birth date for Dad's Mother, Chaya Rachel. She was not included on the website's Family List of 1882, meaning she was born later. And based on the ages of her children she must have been born no earlier than the mid-1880s. Whether Al's educated guess or my sketchy calculations are correct, the span of years between Dad's Mother and her oldest sister would have been considerable.

Finally, after I had turned this book over for publication, I received some of the information I had requested from the U.S. Holocaust Memorial Museum in Washington D.C. The USHMM, after spearheading decades of diplomatic efforts, had finally persuaded the International Tracing Service to make available millions of digital images of arrest, camp, prison, ghetto, and transport records. The ITS is an archive, established after World War II, by the Allies in Bad Arolsen, Germany, to help reunite families separated by the war.

According to the German records, Dad's Mother, "Rachil Pruchno," arrived at Stutthof on July 19, 1944, and was given the concentration camp number 48826. Her birth year was recorded as 1902, which cannot be taken as accurate, for she undoubtedly provided a later year in order to appear younger and therefore more desirable as a worker. The records indicate that five months after her arrival she was admitted to the camp clinic on December 11, 1944, where she died twelve days later, on December 23, 1944, of either a lung infection or inflammation of the intestines. Both were recorded as the cause of death, albeit on three different documents. (The women Yechiel had run into from his hometown said nothing about her being sick, only that her feet froze.) Interestingly, there was a disclaimer at the bottom of two of the documents that stated, "There exists no evidence of any unnatural conditions that occurred in relation to her death." The documents also stated that for hygienic reasons her body was to be cremated immediately. She was, in fact cremated on December 25, Christmas Day.

So far there is no conclusive information on Maša, whose name appeared on the Stutthof registry right underneath her Mother's, as "Musia Sachs," prisoner number 48827. There are no other documents concerning her available at this time. (However, over the next few years, millions more documents are expected to be released by the ITS.) I do so want to see if she died on the same day, and if she died of the same cause. Was "lung infection" really a euphemism for gassed to death? Also of note, and a bit unsettling, the box on the registry indicating "date of death" remained empty for Maša, whereas it had been filled in for her Mother. Was it possible that Yechiel's witnesses were wrong about Maša? Could she have survived Stutthof? If she had, I can't believe she would not have contacted her Uncle Ben in Cleveland to see if he had word of her husband and brothers.

I conclude with the following points of interest concerning Dad and Al's Dachau prisoner registration forms, which the USHMM included along with their Mother's information. Dad claimed to be born in 1924, making him three years older than he really was, again to be more desirable as a worker. Both he and Al stated their occupations as schlosser, which translates as locksmith, toolmaker or metalworker. Also on the form was a fill-in-the-blank physical description for height, body type, facial type, eyes, nose, mouth, ears, hair and teeth. Like a horse, Dad's teeth were noted to be "complete." The documents indicated Dad and Al arrived at Dachau on July 29, 1944. (July 22 was the date noted on Dad's post-war certificate—see chapter *Icking*.) There was even an "arrested on" date, August 15, 1941, which coincides with Dad's memory of moving into the ghetto in mid-August, although the date on Al's document was September 1. Undeniably, the Germans kept meticulous, if somewhat inaccurate, records. As Dad said, "Doing all that paperwork kept the Nazis away from the Russian front."

Todesbescheinigung

Jahr 194.... Nr. des Sterberegisters ....
Eingetragen beim Standesamt Nr. ....

1. Vor- und Zuname: (Bei Kindern ohne Namen, Name des Vaters, ev. bei unehelichen Name der Mutter.)	Rachil Pruchno, geb. Sachs
2. Datum der Geburt: (Bei totgeborenen Kindern das Alter der Frucht)	Jahr 1902. Monat ? Tag ?
3. Geschlecht:	weiblich
4. Stand, Geschäft:	Arbeiterin
5. Wohnung, Strasse, Nr. (eventl. Angabe des Stockwerkes, Hofes od. Kellers)	Schualen
6. Ort des Todes:	K.L Stutthof
7. Tag u. Stunde d. Todes:	23.12.44 um 8,10
8. Krankheit:	Lungenentzündung

Dass ich Obengenannte seit 11.12.44 ärztlich behandelt, die Leiche gesehen und untersucht und an Anzeichen der eingetretenen Verwesung und keine Spur einer unnatürlichen Veranlassung des Todes gefunden habe, bescheinige ich.

Stutthof, den 24. Dezember 4. 194...

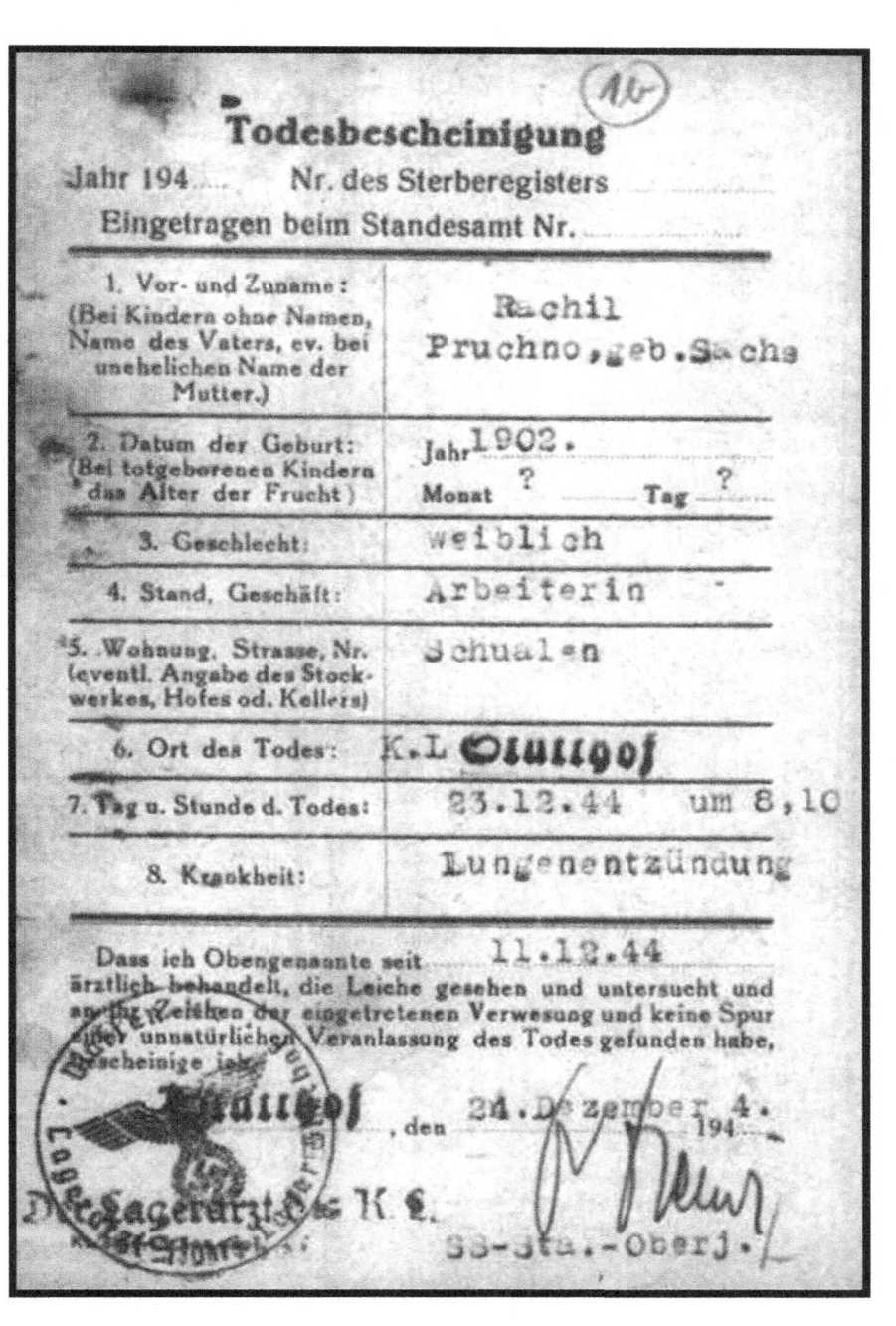

Der Lagerarzt des K.L.
SS-Sta.-Oberj.

Stutthof Death Certificate for Chaya Rachel Pruchno

Dachau paperwork for Sam Pruchno

Konzentrationslager Dachau   Art der Haft: Lit ___   Gef. Nr.: 96018

Name und Vorname: Pruchno Abram
geb.: 6 Mai 1923 zu: Schaulen
Wohnort: Schaulen Rudes 20
Beruf: Schlosser   Rel.: mos
Staatsangehörigkeit: Litauisch   Stand: unverh.
Name der Eltern: Isaak Rachel geb Zak   Rasse: ju
Wohnort: Stutthof
Name der Ehefrau: ___   Rasse: ___
Wohnort: ___
Kinder: ___ Alleiniger Ernährer der Familie oder der Eltern: ___
Vorbildung: ___
Militärdienstzeit: ___ von — bis ___
Kriegsdienstzeit: ___ von — bis ___
Grösse: 1,40   Nase: normal   Haare: braun   Gestalt: ___
Mund: normal   Bart: kein   Gesicht: lang   Ohren: ___
Sprache: litauisch deutsch   Augen: braun   Zähne: 2 fehlt
Ansteckende Krankheit oder Gebrechen: ___
Besondere Kennzeichen: ___
Rentenempfänger: ___
Verhaftet am: 1 Sept 41   wo: Schaulen
1. Mal eingeliefert: 29.7.44   2. Mal eingeliefert: ___
Einweisende Dienststelle: ___
Grund: ___
Parteizugehörigkeit: ___ von — bis ___
Welche Funktionen: ___
Mitglied v. Unterorganisationen: ___
Kriminelle Vorstrafen: ___
Politische Vorstrafen: ___

Ich bin darauf hingewiesen worden, dass meine Bestrafung wegen intellektueller Urkundenfälschung erfolgt, wenn sich die obigen Angaben als falsch erweisen sollten.

v. g. u.   Der Lagerkommandant

Dachau paperwork for Al Pruchno

DAD'S READING RECOMMENDATIONS

Martin Doerry—*My Wounded Heart*

Daniel Jonah Goldhage—*Hitler's Willing Executioners*

Dr. Sheldon Hersh and Dr. Robert Wolf—*The Bugs are Burning*

William W. Mishell—*Kaddish for Kovno*

Michael Selzer—*Deliverance Day: the Last Hours at Dachau*

Major General Sidney Shachnow—*Hope and Honor*

Elie Wiesel—*Night*

ACKNOWLEDGEMENTS

Sam Pruchno, my Dad, for without his willingness to tell his story in infinite detail, this book simply would not have happened. There isn't a single element that has been embellished, if Dad did not say it, I did not write it.

David Kimble, my architecture school friend, who helped me edit this book, hour by hour, word by painstaking word, and always thanked me for the privilege of being involved in what he considered such an important project. He reminded me, and demonstrated to my son, the lengths a true friend will go to help a friend. It sounds cliché, but I honestly could not have done it without his help.

My friends—Joyce Schur, who gave me the confidence to continue on after her initial reading of the first half of the first draft.—Lanie Adair, who read what I thought was the completed manuscript and came up with suggestions that I just couldn't ignore.—Barry Fredman, who helped with the final going over.—Mark Hummel, for translating the German.—Don Griner, for personally going to the USHMM to try to verify information on Dad's sister.—Sharon Meyer, for all things computer related and so much more.

Bob Pruchno, my brother, for his recollections and advice.

Eli Lawrence, my husband, and my son Max too, for their patience with this project, that not only seemed to take forever but actually did.

Thank you all.

Made in the USA
Monee, IL
08 December 2022